Gabler Theses

In der Schriftenreihe „Gabler Theses" erscheinen ausgewählte, englischsprachige Doktorarbeiten, die an renommierten Hochschulen in Deutschland, Österreich und der Schweiz entstanden sind. Die Arbeiten behandeln aktuelle Themen der Wirtschaftswissenschaften und vermitteln innovative Beiträge für Wissenschaft und Praxis. Informationen zum Einreichungsvorgang und eine Übersicht unserer Publikationsangebote finden Sie hier.

Weitere Bände in der Reihe http://www.springer.com/series/16768

Birgit Charlotte Müller

Three Essays on Empirical Asset Pricing in International Equity Markets

Birgit Charlotte Müller
Technische Universität Darmstadt
Darmstadt, Deutschland

Müller, Birgit Charlotte: Three Essays on Empirical Asset Pricing in International Equity
Markets, Darmstadt, Technische Universität Darmstadt, Dissertation
Year of Thesis Publication: 2021
Date of Thesis Defense: 20.05.2021

ISSN 2731-3220   ISSN 2731-3239 (electronic)
Gabler Theses
ISBN 978-3-658-35478-7   ISBN 978-3-658-35479-4 (eBook)
https://doi.org/10.1007/978-3-658-35479-4

Die Deutsche Nationalbibliothek verzeichnet diese Publikation in der Deutschen Nationalbibliografie; detaillierte bibliografische Daten sind im Internet über http://dnb.d-nb.de abrufbar.

Planung/Lektorat: Anna Pietras
Springer Gabler ist ein Imprint der eingetragenen Gesellschaft Springer Fachmedien Wiesbaden
GmbH und ist ein Teil von Springer Nature.
Die Anschrift der Gesellschaft ist: Abraham-Lincoln-Str. 46, 65189 Wiesbaden, Germany

Abstract

This dissertation presents three essays on empirical asset pricing in international equity markets. The first study analyzes the role of firm-specific characteristics for momentum to exist. Reported findings demonstrate that momentum returns can be predicted and enhanced across a wide range of equity markets once combining information of multiple stock characteristics. The study illustrates that both, ordinary and characteristics-enhanced momentum most likely originate from cultural attributes, specifically individualism and power distance. These results make rational explanations of momentum less likely but rather provide empirical support for overreaction-based behavioral theories. The second essay examines the validity, persistence, and robustness of a newly discovered asset pricing factor. Specifically, the study analyzes whether growth in the capital share of aggregate income (GDP) can explain international equity portfolio returns as proposed by Lettau et al. (2019) for the U.S. market. Empirical results show that capital share growth is a priced risk factor across international markets which, however, exhibits severe geographic heterogeneity. Cross-country differences tend to originate from differences in private wealth inequality as well as differences in public wealth and public reserves. Lastly, the third essay analyzes equity market reactions to non-performing loan (NPL) sale announcements. The empirical evidence demonstrates that there exists a significant positive stock market reaction following the announcements of NPL sales. Information related to NPL sale announcements, however, tend to be priced rather quickly within the equity market, implying that there exists only a small time horizon for investors to gain abnormal returns. Reported abnormal returns are driven by a size effect and real estate collateral.

Kurzbeschreibung

Die vorliegende Doktorarbeit präsentiert drei Studien zum Themengebiet der empirischen Kapitalmarktforschung auf Basis internationaler Aktienmärkte. Die erste Studie analysiert den Einfluss firmenspezifischer Charakteristika auf den Momentum-Effekt. Die Ergebnisse der empirischen Untersuchung demonstrieren, dass Momentum-Renditen durch Kombination der Informationen verschiedener Charakteristika vorhergesagt und erhöht werden können. Es wird veranschaulicht, dass sowohl klassische als auch durch Charakteristika erhöhte Momentum-Renditen primär durch kulturelle Eigenschaften wie beispielsweise Individualismus und Machtdistanz erklärt werden können. Diese Ergebnisse lassen rationale Erklärungen des Momentum-Effekts als weniger wahrscheinlich erscheinen und stellen eine empirische Evidenz verhaltensbasierter Theorien dar. Die zweite Studie befasst sich mit der Gültigkeit, Beständigkeit sowie Robustheit eines von Lettau et al. (2019) auf dem US-amerikanischen Markt neu entdeckten Asset Pricing Faktors. Dabei wird untersucht, ob eine Zunahme des relativen Anteils von Kapitaleinkünften am Bruttoinlandsprodukt internationale Aktienportfoliorenditen erklären kann. Die empirische Evidenz belegt, dass dieser Faktor auch für internationale Märkte hohe Relevanz besitzt, gleichzeitig jedoch starke geographische Heterogenität aufweist. Länderunterschiede lassen sich anhand von Unterschieden in der privaten sowie staatlichen Vermögensverteilung sowie staatlichen Gesamtreserven erklären. Schließlich analysiert die dritte Studie die Reaktion internationaler Aktienmärkte auf die Verkaufsankündigung notleidender Kredite (Non-Performing Loans). Die empirischen Ergebnisse belegen, dass eine signifikante positive Aktienmarktreaktion auf die Verkaufsankündigung notleidender Kredite erfolgt. Informationen bezüglich dieser Verkäufe werden von den Aktienmärkten jedoch verhältnismäßig schnell eingepreist. Dies impliziert, dass nur ein geringes Zeitfenster für Investoren existiert, um abnormale Renditen zu generieren. Abnormale Renditen werden von einem Größeneffekt sowie Immobilien als zugrundeliegender Kreditsicherheit getrieben.

Contents

List of Tables

List of Figures

Dedicated to my grandfather and Ingrid

Acknowledgements

This thesis greatly benefitted from the professional and personal guidance, valuable input, and motivating support of my first supervisor, Prof. Dr. Dirk Schiereck. Additionally, I am deeply indebted to my second supervisor, Prof. Dr. Sebastian Müller, for his professional and personal guidance, constant support, valuable input, and encouragement. Most importantly, I would like to express my sincere gratitude to both supervisors for giving me the possibility to conduct this dissertation.

Furthermore, I would like to thank my fellow PhD students at the Technical University of Darmstadt for their helpful comments and suggestions during various PhD seminars. Specifically, I thank Dr. Florian Manz for co-authoring the third study of this dissertation. Part of this thesis was conducted during working periods at the Technical University of Munich and the German Graduate School of Management and Law, at the chair of Prof. Dr. Sebastian Müller. I thank all former colleagues for insightful discussions, comments, and remarks. Beyond, I would like to express my gratitude to multiple anonymous referees, discussants, and participants of conferences and seminars that I attended.

Lastly, I am deeply thankful to my parents, grandparents, Stefanie, Finn, and Benjamin for their unconditional support, trust, and belief in me.

Chapter 1

General Introduction

Asset pricing theory shares the positive versus normative tension present in the rest of economics. Does it describe the way the world does work or the way the world should work?

Cochrane (2009, p. xiii)

© Der/die Autor(en) 2021
B. C. Müller, *Three Essays on Empirical Asset Pricing in International Equity Markets*, Gabler Theses,
https://doi.org/10.1007/978-3-658-35479-4_1

1.1   Motivation and Background

Within the field of capital market research, two diametrically opposed conceptions continue to be prevailing: The efficient market hypothesis by Fama (1970) on the one hand and the behavioral finance approach by Shiller (2003) on the other hand. According to Fama (1970), capital markets are efficient in a sense that current prices of securities incorporate all information available up to that point in time. Consequently, following Fama's reasoning, there exist no possibilities to gain riskless profits by exploiting mispricings (so-called arbitrage) (Fama, 1970). Shiller (2003), in contrast, puts forward the claim that markets tend to behave irrationally, implying that there indeed exist possibilities to exploit mispricings. Those fundamentally different views on the functioning of financial markets as well as concomitant therewith their wide discrepancy, has been highlighted by the fact that both economists have been awarded the Nobel Prize in Economic Sciences in 2013. In 2017, another supporter and co-founder of the behavioral economics approach, Richard Thaler, has been awarded the Nobel Prize in Economic Sciences – emphasizing once more the relevance and topicality of this debate (The Nobel Foundation, 2021).

Central to this ongoing controversy is the existence of return anomalies. Return anomalies are empirical return patterns that cannot be comprehensively explained by existing asset pricing models (Avramov and Chordia, 2006; Brennan and Xia, 2001; Fama and French, 1996). These models range from the traditional capital asset pricing model (CAPM) by Sharpe (1964) and Lintner (1965, 1969), to the three and five factor models by Fama and French (1993, 2015), the four factor model by Carhart (1997), to the more recent q-factors approach by Hou et al. (2015, 2020b), the four factor model by Stambaugh and Yuan (2017), and the behavioral model by Daniel et al. (2020). This range of existing asset pricing models is broad despite being non-exhaustive and continues to grow as a vast amount of new asset pricing factors and anomalies has inundated top finance journals throughout the past decades (Cochrane, 2011; Harvey et al., 2016; Harvey, 2017).

Current research still struggles to justify whether or not the existence of return anomalies can be in line with Fama's efficient market hypothesis. Fama (2014) for instance argues that tests of market efficiency are invariably joint tests of efficiency and the respective asset pricing model used, thus advocating the assumption that anomalies could be explained by the inadequacy of the underlying asset pricing model applied. On the other hand, Shiller (2003) and Thaler (2005) for instance hold the opinion that irrational investor behavior pushes security prices away from fundamental values, as the existence of bubbles and crises within financial markets might indicate likewise.

This positive versus normative tension is illustrated by the introductory quote by Cochrane (2009) cited at the beginning of this chapter: Either existing asset pricing models need improvement or the world is wrong and financial assets are at least partially mispriced. Given the vast amount of newly discovered asset pricing factors and anomalies, this discussion has been augmented by a third dimension which emphasizes severe data mining concerns, implying that many of those recently reported asset pricing factors and anomalies might simply be false and rather driven by the so-called publication bias (Cochrane, 2011; Harvey et al., 2016; Harvey, 2017).

This dissertation contributes to this debate by studying asset pricing anomalies, factors, as well as investor behavior across international equity markets.

1.2   International Equity Markets: An Overview

Within this thesis, international equity markets are considered to be all national equity markets with the exception of the U.S. market. To interact international markets with the U.S., Table 1.1 provides an overview of the ten largest equity markets globally by 2018. Calculations are based upon World Bank data.[1] Markets are ranked in terms of market capitalization of listed domestic companies to aggregate global market capitalization.

Table 1.1: Largest Equity Markets Across the Globe

This table provides an overview of the ten largest stock markets globally as measured by the percental market capitalization of listed domestic companies to worldwide stock market capitalization (Market Cap in % of World) by 2018. Additionally, the table shows the percentage of local GDP to entire world GDP as well as the local market capitalization in percent of local GDP. National currencies are converted to U.S. Dollars.

Country	Market Cap in % of World	Local GDP in % of World	Market Cap in % of Local GDP
United States	43.48%	24.42%	147.89%
China	9.13%	16.28%	45.52%
Japan	7.68%	5.81%	106.90%
Hong Kong	5.51%	0.42%	1055.92%
France	3.48%	3.26%	84.87%
India	3.04%	3.14%	76.79%
Canada	2.75%	1.98%	112.91%
Germany	2.61%	4.65%	44.28%
South Korea	2.03%	1.98%	81.96%
Switzerland	2.03%	0.83%	204.38%

As illustrated within Table 1.1, the U.S. market accounted for approximately 43.48% of global stock market capitalization by 2018, being followed by China (9.13%), and Japan (7.68%). Simultaneously, the U.S. economy represented 24.42% of global GDP, whereas China accounted for 16.28% and Japan for 5.81% of global GDP. Despite their leading role in terms of global percental market capitalization, the U.S. market capitalization constituted only 147.89% of local GDP, whereas this number for instance equalled 1055.92% for Hong

---

[1]Corresponding data is accessible online at https://data.worldbank.org/.

Kong or 204.38% for Switzerland.

These figures exemplify that the U.S. market is still by far the largest equity market in the world. On the other hand, however, the numbers strikingly illustrate that according to World Bank data, almost 60% of the entire stock market capitalization and nearly 75% of global GDP is attributable to international markets. Beyond their importance in terms of economic figures, studying international markets is a worthwhile endeavor for at least the following reasons:

- To test the validity, persistence, and robustness of asset pricing factors and anomalies (Fama and French, 2012, 2017; Jacobs and Müller, 2020)

- To understand what segments and integrates global equity markets (Bekaert et al., 2011; Bekaert and Harvey, 2017; Carrieri et al., 2013)

- To improve regulatory frameworks and market conditions (Albuquerue and Wang, 2008; Hail and Leuz, 2006; Portes and Rey, 2005)

- To identify cross-country differences in investor behavior and their underlying causes (Beugelsdijk and Frijns, 2010; Grinblatt and Keloharju, 2001; Laudenbach et al., 2020)

- To exploit and improve investment strategies (Jacobs and Müller, 2018, 2020; Rizova, 2010)

Despite this economic and scientific importance, the bulk of academic studies up to date still centers on the U.S. market (Karolyi, 2016; Jacobs and Müller, 2020). In fact, Karolyi (2016) finds that only 23% of all empirical studies published in top finance journals focus on non-U.S. markets. This dissertation provides a contribution to this research gap by focusing on empirical asset pricing across international stock markets. The subsequent section provides an overview of the studies comprised within the thesis, summarizes corresponding research questions, underlying data sets used, methodologies applied as well as corresponding main findings.

1.3   Dissertation Studies and Research Questions

This thesis presents three essays on empirical asset pricing in international equity markets. Each essay is a stand-alone empirical study examining the topic from a different angle. The central aspect these essays have in common is that they entirely focus on empirical asset pricing in international equity markets. Figure 1.1 provides an overview of the structure of the thesis and briefly summarizes the topic, data sets, and methodologies of each dissertation study.

Figure 1.1: Overview of Thesis Structure

This figure provides an overview of the main structure of the thesis. Additionally, for each of the three empirical essays, the graph summarizes and contrasts the topic investigated, corresponding data sets used as well as methodologies applied.

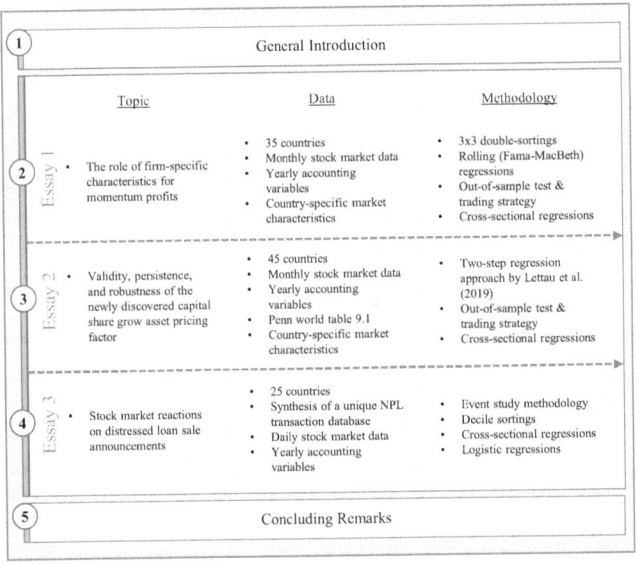

1.3.1 Essay 1: Cross-Country Composite Momentum

The *first essay*[2] (Chapter 2) provides a comprehensive analysis on how firm-specific characteristics relate to the momentum effect. Momentum illustrates the tendency of recent past winner stocks to outperform recent past loser stocks over three to twelve months holding periods (Jegadeesh and Titman, 1993). Researchers have hitherto not reached a consensus on whether this effect can be in line with the efficient market hypothesis by Fama (1970) or whether causes of momentum should be ascribed to irrational investor behavior (Daniel et al., 1998; Hong and Stein, 1999; Li, 2018; Vayanos and Woolley, 2013). More recently, several academic studies have started to analyze the role of stock characteristics for momentum to exist (Da et al., 2014; Hillert et al., 2014; Sagi and Seasholes, 2007; Zhang, 2006). The rationale beyond is that certain attributes may indicate if a stock is prone to behavioral biases or that certain characteristics may signal specific risk features. As a result, a substantial amount of complex interaction patterns has emerged, with the underlying causes inconsistently subsumed by prior research. Given this fragmentation and disparity, the research questions addressed within the first dissertation study are as follows:

1. Do stock characteristics have true power in enhancing and thus explaining momentum returns?

2. Which characteristics are the most consistent drivers of momentum?

3. Are there differences or commonalities across countries and regions worldwide?

4. What explains potential geographic heterogeneity?

The study implements a 35 country-level analysis of 18 stock characteristics between January 1989 and June 2019 to answer these research questions. The results show that momentum profits can be predicted and enhanced across many international markets when combining information of these stock characteristics. Predicted momentum profits can yield significant positive out-of-sample portfolio returns which cannot be explained by idiosyncratic volatility, extreme past returns or Carhart's four factors to their full extent. Applying cross-sectional

---

[2]This chapter is based on the following working paper: Müller, B. and Müller, S. (2020). Cross-Country Composite Momentum. Available online at SSRN.

regression analyses, the study identifies that both, ordinary and characteristics-enhanced momentum returns originate from behavioral biases. Specifically, the study shows that global differences can best be explained by cultural differences as proxied by the six cultural dimensions of Hofstede (2011).

1.3.2   Essay 2: Capital Share Risk in International Asset Pricing

The *second essay*[3] (Chapter 3) examines the validity, persistence, and robustness of a newly discovered asset pricing factor. Specifically, the study analyzes whether growth in the capital share (KS) of aggregate income (GDP) is a priced risk factor across international equity markets as proposed by Lettau et al. (2019) for the U.S. market. Within their paper, Lettau et al. (2019) exemplify that this single factor outperforms, and even subsumes, information in prominent and well-established asset pricing models. Therefore, the second dissertation study strives to answer the following research questions:

1. Is capital share growth a persistent and consistent driver of equity portfolio returns across global equity markets?

2. Are there differences and commonalities across countries and regions worldwide? What explains potential cross-country differences?

3. Is it possible to exploit the information contained in the capital share growth factor by a tradable (out-of-sample) investment strategy?

The analysis concentrates on 45 equity markets between January 1989 and December 2017. Following the two-step regression approach by Lettau et al. (2019), the empirical evidence demonstrates that capital share growth is a priced risk factor across international markets which, however, exhibits strong geographic heterogeneity. Pooled estimates show that capital share growth is particularly significant for Emerging Markets, while being less relevant for G7 + Australia (excl. U.S. market). Unlike the U.S., the information contained in the

---

[3]This chapter is based on the following working paper: Müller, B., Müller, S., and Schiereck, D. (2021). Capital Share Risk in International Asset Pricing. Available online at SSRN.

KS factor of international markets does not subsume information contained in alternative factor models, but partly adds additional explanatory content to these model specifications. Furthermore, the analysis identifies that capital share growth is a local rather than global asset pricing factor given that the explanatory power is substantially reduced once applying global rather than local risk estimates. Country differences are found to originate from variations in private wealth inequality as well as differences in public wealth and public reserves. Lastly, the study illustrates that the information contained in the capital share growth factor cannot be exploited by an out-of-sample investment strategy despite strong in-sample explanatory power.

1.3.3 Essay 3: The Pricing of European Non-Performing Real Estate Loan Portfolios

The *third essay*[4] (Chapter 4) studies how European equity markets react upon distressed loan sale announcements. Distressed loans, also referred to as non-performing loans (NPL), are risky and complex bank assets that to a large extent tend to be collateralized by real estate (Fell et al., 2017). Several recent academic studies, however, have detected severe problems of financial market participants in the pricing of real estate financial products (Cici et al., 2011; Mori and Ziobrowski, 2011; Woltering et al., 2018). The third study contributes to this literature stream by addressing the following research questions:

1. How do capital market participants evaluate complex asset sales whose cash flows are heavily dependent on real estate income?

2. To what extent can potentially abnormal returns be explained upon the basis of vendor characteristics?

3. Which institutions take the risk involved in those sold portfolios?

To answer these questions, a unique data set for distressed loan sales from European vendor banks is synthesized from 2012 to 2018. This data set is applied to provide summary

---

[4]This chapter is based on the following publication: Manz, F., Müller, B., and Schiereck, D. (2020). The pricing of European non-performing real estate loan portfolios: Evidence on stock market evaluation of complex asset sales. Journal of Business Economics, 90:1087-1120.

statistics on the European NPL market, which thus far lacks transparency and publicly available information. Next, provided that corresponding banks are publicly traded, event study methodology is used to examine short-term valuation effects following NPL sale announcements. The results provide robust evidence in favor of a significant positive stock market reaction at vendor banks following NPL sales. Cross-sectional regression analysis reveals that positive market reactions are driven by a size effect and real estate collateral. Lastly, using logistic regression analysis, the study shows that real estate NPLs are most often acquired by opportunistic funds, while they are avoided by consortia of multiple buyers and undisclosed investors. The study attributes these findings to the specific characteristics of real estate as an asset class and the specific knowledge and human resources needed by investors to cope with it.

Subsequently, the three dissertation studies are presented in detail. The final chapter (Chapter 5) provides a summary of the thesis' main findings and delivers a final conclusion.

Chapter 2

Cross-Country Composite Momentum

This chapter presents the first dissertation study which investigates the role of firm-specific characteristics for momentum to exist.

Zusatzmaterial online
Zusätzliche Informationen sind in der Online-Version dieses Kapitel (https://doi.org/10.1007/978-3-658-35479-4_2) enthalten.

B. C. Müller, *Three Essays on Empirical Asset Pricing in International Equity Markets*, Gabler Theses,
https://doi.org/10.1007/978-3-658-35479-4_2

2.1   Introduction

Medium-term price continuation, commonly defined as momentum, is a widespread phenomenon in financial markets. It exists for individual stocks (Jegadeesh and Titman, 1993), for industry sectors (Moskowitz and Grinblatt, 1999), for style portfolios (Lewellen, 2002), in international equity markets (Rouwenhorst, 1998; Chui et al., 2010), and across asset classes (Bhojraj and Swaminathan, 2006; Menkhoff et al., 2012; Asness et al., 2013). Momentum also appears to be persistent over time, at least outside the U.S. stock market (Jegadeesh and Titman, 2001; McLean and Pontif, 2016; Green et al., 2017; Jacobs and Müller, 2020). Momentum strategies generate substantial long-short returns on paper, and they constitute an apparent violation of the efficient market hypothesis in its weak form (Fama, 1970). Hence, it is arguably not surprising that several theoretical approaches serve to explain the existence of momentum (Barberis et al., 1998; Daniel et al., 1998; Hong and Stein, 1999; Lee and Swaminathan, 2000; Vayanos and Woolley, 2013).

To test these competing momentum explanations empirically, a long strand of literature (Hong et al., 2000; Lee and Swaminathan, 2000; Zhang, 2006; Verardo, 2009; Da et al., 2014; Hillert et al., 2014) has analyzed the role of stock characteristics to potentially act as momentum "enhancing" drivers. As a result, a substantial amount of complex interaction patterns has emerged for momentum, with the underlying causes inconsistently subsumed by prior research. Explanation attempts vary from behavioral, limits-to-arbitrage to rational risk-based approaches, mirroring the wide range of existing theories on underyling causes of ordinary momentum itself.

Given this fragmentation and disparity in the enhanced momentum literature, our study aims to take a comprehensive and global perspective on how stock characteristics relate to momentum returns. While prior academic studies have focused on causes of global differences in ordinary momentum returns (e.g. Chui et al. (2010)), international studies upon (sources of) enhanced momentum have been neglected thus far. We believe that testing for sources of global differences in enhanced momentum, though, can offer valuable insights on the validity of theoretical explanations for ordinary momentum itself.

The rationale of our study is as follows. First, our study aims to be the first to analyze and document the existence, magnitude, and distribution of enhanced momentum returns across international equity markets. In this regard, we apply a wide range of stock characteristics which have been shown empirically to function as momentum enhancers and which have been published in top tier finance journals. Second, we combine the information of various firm-specific attributes within a single momentum enhancer at a time and test for the profitability of an investment strategy that takes advantage of our metric's information density. We refer to this metric as composite-momentum enhancer. Lastly, we strive to identify causes for global differences in both, ordinary and composite-enhanced momentum returns by applying a variety of country characteristics that serve as proxies for theoretical momentum explanations as outlined in Section 2.2. In doing so, we simultaneously analyze whether there exists a common root cause for ordinary momentum and composite-enhanced momentum returns.

To address these questions, we implement a 35 country-level analysis of 18 stock characteristics to test for their ability to enhance and predict momentum profits. Tested characteristics are based on a comprehensive review of the enhanced momentum literature and include: size, r-squared, turnover, age, analyst coverage, forecast dispersion, book-to-market, price, illiquidity, capital gains, information diffusion, failure probability, maximum daily return, equity duration, 52-week high price, asset growth, costs of goods sold, and revenue volatility.

Empirical findings provide evidence on the relevance of characteristics in enhancing momentum returns in international markets. The explanatory power to a large extent maintains after accounting for idiosyncratic volatility and extreme past returns as emphasized by Bandarchuk and Hilscher (2013). This finding reassures many of the conclusions taken from earlier momentum enhancing work. Out of a set of eighteen stock characteristics, we find particularly age, book-to-market, maximum daily return, R^2, information diffusion, and 52-week high or low price to matter for momentum profits. Intuitively, the importance of these characteristics seems consistent with behavioral explanation attempts as momentum appears to be stronger for hard-to-value firms (young firms with a low book-to-market ratio) with high information uncertainty (low R^2), and when investors are prone to underreaction (information diffusion; nearness to 52-week highs and lows). Beyond, our insights imply that a modest link between past returns, stock volatility, and momentum profits itself cannot explain enhanced momentum to its full extent.

To test if the link between momentum and stock characteristics is systematic and persistent, we analyze out-of-sample whether momentum profits can be predicted upon the basis of a composite-momentum metric. Specifically, we run rolling monthly multivariate regressions of momentum profits on characteristics. By applying average regression coefficients and constants on a five-year rolling basis, we use fitted values to predict momentum profits for the following month. When running univariate Fama and MacBeth (1973) regressions, we find that our predicted momentum measure is statistically significant at the 1%-level in explaining actual momentum profits, within 27 of our 35 countries investigated. Further, a momentum-neutral investment strategy that double-sorts on predicted momentum and past returns delivers monthly returns of 0.88% for the U.S. market (t-statistics: 3.13) and 1.14% for our international sample (t-statistics: 5.27). The statistical significance remains after accounting for idiosyncratic volatility and extreme past returns. Our findings thus suggest a strong and systematic link between firm-specific attributes and momentum.

We contribute to existing research in three ways. First, we add to the long-standing controversy on the behavioral versus rational debate of the underlying causes of momentum. Researchers have hitherto not reached a consensus on whether momentum can be ascribed to either rational or irrational investor behavior. Stock characteristics have become central to this controversy as they have proven to operate as momentum drivers. We add to this literature by providing empirical evidence that stock characteristics indeed have power in enhancing and even predicting momentum returns. Our cross-country analyses imply that both, ordinary and composite-enhanced momentum returns tend to be higher within countries that exhibit less trading frictions (i.e. developed markets with no short-sale constraints) and markets that exhibit less information opaqueness. This implies that ordinary and composite-enhanced momentum returns are higher whenever we observe markets with clear and easily accessible information. Simultaneously, we find composite-enhanced momentum returns to be higher in highly individualistic countries that simultaneously exhibit smaller degrees of power distance. Multivariate regressions reveal that our proxies for cultural differences are stronger and more significant in explaining both, ordinary and composite-enhanced momentum returns as opposed to proxies for market efficiency or slow information diffusion.

Second, we contribute to the general anomaly literature which has reemphasized data mining concerns recently (Lewellen et al., 2010; Cochrane, 2011; Harvey et al., 2016; Hou et al., 2020a). Specifically, by applying a (country, characteristics) 35x18 analysis, we conduct a broad international out-of-sample test and are able to detect which of the chosen characteristics are indeed major momentum enhancers across countries worldwide. This is relevant given that the importance of all of our chosen characteristics was originally detected by applying U.S. level data. Our study provides novel evidence on the robustness of our chosen set of characteristics in enhancing cross-sectional momentum returns. Overall, for the enhanced momentum literature our results do not suggest that "most claimed research findings...are likely false" (Harvey et al., 2016, p. 5). Rather, the momentum enhancing role of several characteristics such as firm age appears to be a consistent and persistent phenomenon in worldwide equity markets. This finding makes a data mining explanation for momentum less likely, but rather provides supportive evidence for behavioral explanation attempts (Barberis et al., 1998; Daniel et al., 1998; Hong and Stein, 1999).

Lastly, our insights have implications for the growing literature on international stock market segmentations. Results reported by former international out-of-sample tests concerning the ordinary momentum anomaly as conducted by Griffin et al. (2003), Chui et al. (2010), or Asness et al. (2013) often find substantial cross-country differences. Other studies related to the anomaly literature as the ones by Rapach et al. (2013) or Jacobs and Müller (2020) also detect geographic stock market segmentations. Our findings reveal apparently striking evidence for regional patterns between North America, Pacific, Europe, and Emerging Markets. Even within these regions, though, in part we still find a large variability of the importance of stock characteristics. While particular characteristics may not be a momentum enhancer in one country, they may play a big role in other, geographically related markets. From a practical perspective, this insight is also important for investors.

The paper proceeds as follows. Section 2.2 gives a brief overview of related literature and places our work within the current state of research. In Section 2.3, we outline the data set underlying our analysis, our construction of composite-momentum, and measurement of return dispersion. Section 2.4 reports our baseline results obtained from dependent double-sorting techniques and Fama-MacBeth regressions. In Section 2.5, we conduct cross-country analyses and illustrate drivers of global differences for both, ordinary and composite-enhanced momentum returns. Section 2.6 summarizes insights obtained from our study and concludes.

2.2   An Overview on Momentum Models and Enhanced Momentum Strategies

Existing theories on the underlying drivers of momentum are conflicting. For instance, Berk et al. (1999), Johnson (2002), Li (2018) as well as Vayanos and Woolley (2013) provide explanations complying with Fama's rational asset pricing paradigm.[1] Conversely, Barberis et al. (1998), Chan et al. (1996), Daniel et al. (1998), Hong and Stein (1999) as well as more recently Docherty and Hurst (2018) deliver plausible behavioral theories.[2]

Berk et al. (1999) argue that momentum results from changes in a firm's assets and growth options, leading to conditional expected returns. Johnson (2002) complements the work by Berk et al. (1999) by emphasizing that stochastic growth rates arising out of a time-varying exposure to firm-specific projects, account for momentum returns. Opposed to these firm-specific perspectives, Vayanos and Woolley (2013) emphasize the role of active fund flows in explaining momentum. Within their theoretical work, momentum arises if fund flows exhibit inertia and prices underreact to expected future flows. Gradual fund flows are assumed to be either driven by investor inertia or institutional constraints and are expected to be higher among high idiosyncratic volatility assets. More recently, Li (2018) establishes a neoclassical investment-based model arguing that productivity shocks, relative price shocks (indicating variations in the price of investment goods relative to that of consumption goods) as well as

---

[1] A non-exhaustive list on further explanations fitting rational asset pricing theory comprise works by Carhart (1997), Conrad and Kaul (1998), Chordia and Shivakumar (2002), Makarov and Rytchkov (2012), Barroso and Santa-Clara (2015), Daniel and Moskowitz (2016), Min and Kim (2016) as well as Maio and Philip (2018).

[2] Other behavioral attempts are for instance reported by Grinblatt and Han (2005), Baker and Wurgler (2007), and Banerjee et al. (2009).

investment frictions constitute underlying drivers of both, momentum returns and the value premium.

Contrarily, Chan et al. (1996) state that momentum results from a gradual diffusion of information into the market, particularly earnings-related news. Relatedly, Barberis et al. (1998) argue that momentum arises from the initial underreaction of a representative investor to news due to psychological biases such as representativeness and conservatism. The approach induced by Hong and Stein (1999) implies that information on a stock's fundamental value diffuses only gradually into the market. Hong and Stein (1999) distinguish between two types of investors: news watchers and momentum traders. News watchers underreact to new information, leading prices to adjust too slowly. Momentum traders exploiting these patterns in turn generate overreactions, leading to long-term reversals. In a similar manner, Docherty and Hurst (2018) argue that momentum is driven by myopic investors who overweight public information, leading to a slow diffusion of fundamental news. According to Docherty and Hurst (2018), myopic investment behavior is driven by short-term incentives as well as investor perceptions of other investors' beliefs similar to the beauty contest metaphor of Keynes (1936). Daniel et al. (1998) deliver a model in which momentum stems from intermediate market overreactions. Overconfidence and biased self-attribution causes investors to overweight (underweight) public information confirming (contradicting) their private stock evaluations. As uncertainty rises, psychological biases and thus mispricings are assumed to be strengthened.[3]

To test these competing explanations for the momentum effect empirically, numerous scholars have analyzed the ability of stock characteristics[4] to function as momentum enhancers. The rationale beyond is that certain firm attributes may indicate if a stock is prone to investor overreaction or underreaction (such as being "hard-to-value") or that certain firm attributes may signal specific risk features associated with momentum (such as suffering from "crash

---

[3]Still, one might argue that deviations from fundamentals should instantly be arbitraged away by investors exploiting mispricings. Earlier works (De Long et al., 1990; Shleifer and Vishny, 1997; Barberis et al., 1998) stress that because investor sentiments are at least partially unpredictable, arbitrageurs bear the risk of losing money in the short run, thus preventing them from pushing prices back to their fundamentals.

[4]Apart from firm-specific characteristics, another strand of literature analyzes macroeconomic aspects for momentum to exist. For instance, Avramov et al. (2016) study aggregate market liquidity whereas Min and Kim (2016) study economic downside risk.

risk"). Thus, to the extent this logic holds, conditioning on such firm-specific attributes should yield higher momentum returns. In the following, we refer to these studies as enhanced momentum literature.

In the enhanced momentum literature a large body of firm-specific attributes has been examined to test the validity of existing momentum theories. Empirical evidence is reported for characteristics such as size (Hong et al., 2000; Zhang, 2006), past trading volume (Lee and Swaminathan, 2000), analyst coverage (Hong et al., 2000; Zhang, 2006), age (Zhang, 2006), credit rating (Avramov et al., 2007), revenue volatility (Sagi and Seasholes, 2007), information diffusion (Da et al., 2014), and media coverage (Hillert et al., 2014).[5] Prior literature majorly attributes return enhancing abilities of characteristics to behavioral momentum theories. Still, empirical findings verify and augment opposing models. The difficulty lies in disentangling the sole effect of firm-specific attributes in enhancing momentum returns. Interaction patterns are complex and might either stem from the specific attribute itself, correlations with a multitude of other characteristics, omitted factors, or simply be interpreted in a variety of ways to either proxy for rational or behavioral theories, for market under- or overreactions.

Empirical evidence for the slow information diffusion model by Hong and Stein (1999) is for instance provided by Hong et al. (2000) and Avramov et al. (2007). Findings reported by Hoberg and Phillips (2018) are consistent with both, the model by Hong and Stein (1999) as well as the one proposed by Barberis et al. (1998). Contrarily, studies conducted by Zhang (2006), Chui et al. (2010), Hillert et al. (2014) as well as Avramov et al. (2016) rather provide support for the behavioral theory induced by Daniel et al. (1998). Sagi and Seasholes (2007) attribute their enhanced momentum findings to rational models proposed by Berk et al. (1999) and Johnson (2002) while, however, not exclusively precluding behavioral attempts. Beyond, works by Lee and Swaminathan (2000), George and Hwang (2004) as well as Da et al. (2014) do not fit neatly into existing frameworks, thus rather deliver own explanations for reported interaction patterns.

---

[5] A non-exhaustive list on further momentum-enhancing strategies include studies on illiquidity (Amihud, 2002), 52-week high price (George and Hwang, 2004), unrealized capital gains (Grinblatt and Han, 2005), R^2 (Hou et al., 2006), dispersion in analyst forecasts of earnings (Verardo, 2009), maximum daily return (Jacobs et al., 2016), and industry-based economic links (Hoberg and Phillips, 2018).

Instead of relating enhanced momentum returns to existing rational or behavioral theories, Bandarchuk and Hilscher (2013) offer an unprecedented explanation approach for why firm-specific attributes can be used to increase momentum returns. A major point of criticism invoked by them is that the bulk of previous enhanced momentum literature has centered on characteristics one at a time while characteristics tend to be correlated with each other as well as with past returns and idiosyncratic volatility.

Bandarchuk and Hilscher (2013, p. 824) argue that "recent winners are more likely to have high volatility. If volatility and characteristics are correlated, recent winners and losers have more extreme characteristics." They therefore stress that sorting on characteristics and past returns implies a hidden double-sort on volatility and past returns. A hidden sorting on volatility, in turn, implies a sort on more extreme past returns. Following this reasoning, double-sorting stocks on characteristics and past returns is assumed to lead to enhanced momentum returns solely due to this correlation. In line with this argumentation, the explanatory power of stock characteristics is expected to be substantially reduced once controlling for this effect. Bandarchuk and Hilscher (2013, p. 811) thus "suggest that a focus on the link between extreme past returns and momentum profits may be more appropriate." To the extent this reasoning holds, it poses a challenge for both, existing rational and behavioral momentum theories.[6]

Given this fragmentation and disparity in the enhanced momentum literature, our study aims to take a comprehensive and global perspective on how stock characteristics relate to momentum returns. While prior academic studies have focused on causes of global differences in ordinary momentum returns (e.g. Chui et al. (2010)), international studies upon (sources of) enhanced momentum have been neglected thus far. We believe that testing for sources of global differences in enhanced momentum, though, can offer valuable insights on the validity of theoretical explanations for ordinary momentum itself.

The rationale of our study is as follows. First, we aim to analyze and document the existence, magnitude, and distribution of enhanced momentum returns across international equity markets. In this regard, we apply previously reported stock characteristics which

---

[6]As remarked by Bandarchuk and Hilscher (2013), the theory closest to their logic is the one proposed by Vayanos and Woolley (2013) since they link momentum to high idiosyncratic volatility assets.

have been shown empirically to function as momentum enhancers and which have been published in top tier finance journals. Additionally, we account for potential interdependencies as reported by Bandarchuk and Hilscher (2013).

Second, we combine the information of various firm-specific attributes within a single momentum enhancer at a time and test for the profitability of an investment strategy that takes advantage of our metric's information density.

Lastly, we strive to identify causes for global differences in both, ordinary and composite-enhanced momentum returns by applying a variety of country characteristics that serve as proxies for theoretical momentum explanations as outlined in Section 2.2. In doing so, we simultaneously analyze whether there exists a common root cause for ordinary momentum and enhanced momentum returns.

2.3   Data and Methodology

2.3.1   Stock Market Data

We derive our data set from Datastream/Worldscope. The database is commonly employed for studies on momentum in international markets (Chui et al., 2010; Fama and French, 2012; Asness et al., 2013). Our sample period runs from January 1989 to June 2019. The initial starting date is the same as in the international study of Fama and French (2012) and illustrates a trade-off between maximizing the length of the time-series and maximizing the number of countries that can be included in the analysis. For some international markets, the starting date might vary due to availability of market data on Datastream or because of our screening criteria outlined in the following.

Stocks that at the beginning of each month are contained within the lowest NYSE market capitalization decile are excluded from our study. Following prior literature (Chui et al., 2010), this step ensures that momentum returns are not exclusively driven by small and illiquid stocks. To mitigate for the effect of outliers, returns are winsorized at the 0.1% and

99.9% levels. Each month, for each country we require at least 90 stocks to be available.[7] We justify this approach by the need of having sufficient observations to double-sort stocks into portfolios. If there are less than 180 months left fulfilling the criteria of 90 stocks or above for a country, we exclude the respective country from our analysis. We use a threshold of 180 months to ensure a minimum time-series of ten years within subsequent out-of-sample tests for which a lead time of 60 months is required as further outlined in Section 2.3.2.2.

Starting with 68 countries worldwide, our filtering criteria lead to a final sub-sample of thirty-five countries. The final countries included based of sufficient data availability are: Australia, Belgium, Brazil, Canada, Chile, China, Denmark, Finland, France, Germany, Greece, Hong Kong, Indonesia, India, Italy, Japan, Malaysia, Mexico, Netherlands, Norway, New Zealand, Pakistan, Philippines, Poland, Singapore, South Africa, South Korea, Spain, Sweden, Switzerland, Taiwan, Thailand, Turkey, United Kingdom, and United States.[8] Taken all countries together, our final sample contains a total of 59,734 stocks of which 11,499 can be ascribed to the U.S. market.

Table 2.1 summarizes how firms and ordinary momentum returns are distributed among countries. Ordinary momentum returns are calculated going long the tertile of past return winners and short the tertile of past return losers. Excluding the most recent month, we use a six months period to calculate past returns and establish the momentum portfolios.

As shown in Table 2.1, largest country samples are obtained for the U.S. (11,499 firms), Japan (5,537 firms), and Canada (4,868 firms). The smallest sub-samples include New Zealand (186 firms), Mexico (202 firms), and Finland (225 firms). The worldwide percental market value (as of June 2019) accordingly is highest for the U.S. (38.20%), China (10.72%), and Japan (7.57%).

---

[7]This number constitutes a trade-off between maximizing the number of countries in the analysis and ensuring a minimum number of stocks within the enhanced momentum portfolios for reasons of liquidity and reliability. When applying 3x3 sorting technique, we are able to ensure an initial minimum number of 10 stocks within each sub-portfolio.

[8]In total, these 35 countries represent 95.07% of the total market capitalization of the larger pool of our initial 68 countries as of June 2019.

Table 2.1: Summary Statistics: Data Sample and Ordinary Momentum Returns

This table provides an overview of how firms and classical momentum profits are distributed among countries. We report the total absolute number of months, the total absolute number of firms as well as the average number of firms per month on a country-basis. We also state a country's worldwide percental market value as of June 2019. Additionally, we indicate summary statistics of ordinary momentum returns per country. We report mean, skewness, kurtosis, and sharpe ratios (SR) respectively. Ordinary momentum returns are calculated going long the tertile of past return winners and short the tertile of past return losers, indicating realized returns in t+1. Excluding the most recent month, we use a six months period to calculate past returns and establish the momentum portfolios. Sharpe ratios are annualized and computed using time-series averages of monthly momentum profits, risk-free rates, and standard deviations. The internationally pooled sample (International) contains all of our chosen countries apart from the U.S. market. Our sample period runs from M1:1989 to M6:2019. *, **, and *** indicate statistical significance at the 10%, 5%, and 1% level.

| Country | Abbrev. | Data Sample | | | | | Ordinary Momentum | | | |
		Beginning Month	Total Anomaly Months	Total # Firms	Average # Firms Per Month	% Market Value	Mean	Skew	Kurt	Sharpe Ratio
Australia	atl	01/1989	366	3,139	220.24	1.85%	1.16%***	-0.69	6.49	0.26
Belgium	bel	06/1997	265	231	60.82	0.49%	1.15%***	-0.33	7.09	0.21
Brazil	bra	06/2000	229	279	93.18	0.92%	1.19%***	-1.25	9.28	0.18
Canada	can	01/1989	366	4,868	338.40	2.73%	0.96%***	-1.08	8.41	0.17
Chile	chi	06/1998	242	241	71.25	0.30%	0.70%**	-1.77	11.07	0.14
China	chn	06/1996	277	3,877	1,392.16	10.72%	-0.29%	0.10	4.73	-0.11
Denmark	den	11/1989	356	325	53.29	0.50%	1.14%***	0.06	4.90	0.22
Finland	fin	06/1997	265	225	56.27	0.37%	0.35%	-0.54	5.20	0.04
France	fra	01/1989	366	1,743	276.53	3.61%	0.54%**	0.41	17.65	0.07
Germany	ger	06/1989	361	1,557	199.09	2.60%	0.67%***	-0.01	10.82	0.09
Greece	gre	06/1994	301	390	54.26	0.06%	0.71%	-1.35	14.62	0.06
Hong Kong	hkg	12/1990	343	2,288	318.80	4.42%	0.55%**	-1.92	12.26	0.07
Indonesia	ido	06/1993	308	687	89.52	0.65%	0.15%	-0.76	12.83	-0.01
India	ind	09/1992	322	3,708	273.15	2.88%	0.86%***	-1.46	13.25	0.12
Italy	ita	01/1989	366	622	138.92	0.87%	0.54%**	-0.05	9.18	0.07
Japan	jap	01/1989	366	5,537	1,426.32	7.57%	-0.16%	-0.72	9.41	-0.10
Malaysia	mal	09/1991	334	1,342	153.28	0.51%	0.53%	-6.29	77.71	0.05
Mexico	mex	06/1999	241	202	74.00	0.47%	0.71%**	-1.36	9.91	0.12
Netherlands	net	01/1989	366	313	81.87	0.79%	0.66%***	-0.22	5.68	0.09
Norway	nor	06/1994	301	516	72.02	0.41%	1.04%***	0.01	4.46	0.17
New Zealand	nzl	12/2001	206	186	35.04	0.14%	1.08%***	0.65	6.75	0.27
Pakistan	pak	06/2000	229	283	32.81	0.04%	0.79%**	-0.16	6.75	0.11
Philippines	phi	06/1996	277	294	55.19	0.36%	0.22%	-2.18	19.07	0.01
Poland	pol	06/2001	210	707	60.62	0.21%	1.11%***	-0.76	6.30	0.20
Singapore	sin	06/1992	325	1,084	132.20	0.78%	0.44%	-2.76	22.92	0.05
South Africa	soa	01/1990	354	857	116.20	0.65%	0.78%***	-0.64	5.05	0.12
South Korea	sok	06/1990	349	2,826	227.25	1.66%	0.33%	-0.99	14.70	0.02
Spain	spa	06/1990	349	370	93.70	1.00%	0.59%**	-0.98	8.99	0.08
Sweden	swe	06/1990	349	1,031	103.01	0.82%	0.58%**	-0.56	8.33	0.07
Switzerland	swi	01/1989	366	411	130.78	2.19%	0.91%***	-0.68	8.79	0.18
Taiwan	tai	06/1995	289	2,362	298.09	1.41%	0.28%	-1.14	8.79	0.02
Thailand	tha	01/1989	325	918	105.08	0.73%	0.61%	-2.27	17.10	0.05
Turkey	tur	06/1998	253	453	74.81	0.18%	-0.15%	-0.75	5.93	-0.06
United Kingdom	uni	01/1989	366	4,363	552.96	3.99%	0.93%***	-1.17	14.60	0.17
United States	usa	01/1989	366	11,499	2,411.37	38.20%	0.34%	-0.95	15.96	0.02
International	internat	01/1989	366	48,235	6,696.22	56.87%	0.50%**	-0.52	5.42	0.06

Lowest percental market values are reported for Pakistan (0.04%), Greece (0.06%), and New Zealand (0.14%). Average median market value per month ranges from lowest 521.95 million USD (Pakistan) to highest 1,486.77 million USD (Spain). Our internationally pooled sample comprising all of our sample countries with the exception of the U.S., contains 48,235 companies and illustrates 56.87% of worldwide percental market value as of June 2019. Ordinary monthly momentum returns on average are highest for Brazil (1.19%), Australia (1.16%), and Belgium (1.15%) and lowest for China (-0.29%), Japan (-0.16%), and Turkey (-0.15%). Within the U.S., ordinary momentum strategies yield average monthly returns of 0.34% with a standard deviation of 4.72%. At an internationally pooled basis, we obtain average monthly momentum returns of 0.50% with a standard deviation of 4.54%.

Overall, ordinary momentum returns tend to be negatively skewed, ranging from -6.29 (Malaysia) to -0.01 (Germany). Within Norway, Denmark, China, France, and New Zealand, though, monthly momentum returns are even slightly positively skewed, ranging from 0.01 (Norway) to 0.65 (New Zealand). Skewness of the U.S. amounts to -0.95, whereas it amounts to -0.52 for our internationally pooled sample. Our findings are in line with prior research, indicating for instance that momentum strategies do not tend to perform well within Asian countries (Griffin et al., 2003; Chui et al., 2010). Furthermore, in line with existing studies, we find that momentum returns tend to attenuate within the U.S. market (Barroso and Santa-Clara, 2015; Daniel and Moskowitz, 2016). At an internationally pooled level, we observe a comparatively stable trend of momentum across time.

2.3.2 Composite Momentum

2.3.2.1 Selection and Measurement of Momentum-Enhancing Characteristics

To construct our composite momentum enhancer, we combine a variety of firm-specific attributes. Out of the anomaly literature, we choose a set of eighteen stock characteristics, most of which have been published in leading finance journals. Table 2.2 provides an overview of applied characteristics, their predicted way of interaction with momentum returns, respective reference studies as well as variable definitions.

Table 2.2: Overview of Applied Characteristics

This table summarizes characteristics applied within our analysis to enhance momentum profits, predicted momentum signs (whether or not expected correlations with momentum profits are either positive or negative), corresponding reference studies, and variable definitions, respectively.

Characteristic	Abbrev.	Sign	Reference Study	Definition
size	size	-	Hong et al. (2000)	market value of equity in USD
r-squared	R^2	-	Hou et al. (2006)	fraction of a firms return variance explained by the market factor
turnover	turn	+	Lee and Swaminathan (2000)	shares traded per month divided by the number of shares outstanding
age	age	-	Zhang (2006)	number of years, based on a firm's first appearance in Datastream
analyst coverage	nanalyst	+	Hong et al. (2000)	number of analysts covering stock
forecast dispersion	eps-disp	+	Zhang (2006)	dispersion in forecasted EPS
book-to-market	bm	-	Asness (1997)	book value of equity/market value of equity
price	price	+	Bandarchuk and Hilscher (2013)	price index not adjusted for stock splits in US-Dollar
illiquidity	illiquid	+	Amihud (2002)	average daily ratio of absolute stock return to dollar volume
failure probability	failure	+	Campbell et al. (2011)	financial distress measure
capital gains	cgs	+	Grinblatt and Han (2005)	capital gains of stock over previous five years
information diffusion	ID	-	Da et al. (2014)	continuous information proxy/continuous information arrival
maximum daily return	max-ret	-	Jacobs et al. (2016)	a stock's maximum daily return over the past one month
equity duration	dur	+	Dechow et al. (2004)	average maturity of a stock's expected future cash flows
52-week high price	P52-WH	+	George and Hwang (2004)	ratio of the current stock price to the maximum stock price of past 52 weeks
asset growth	ag	+	Cooper et al. (2008)	year-on-year percentage change in total assets
costs of goods sold	cogs	+	Sagi and Seasholes (2007)	costs of goods sold divided by a firms total assets
revenue volatility	rev-vola	+	Sagi and Seasholes (2007)	standard deviation of a stocks revenue growth throughout the past five years

As illustrated, we account for size (Hong et al., 2000), r-squared (Hou et al., 2006), turnover (Lee and Swaminathan, 2000), age (Zhang, 2006), analyst coverage (Hong et al., 2000), forecast dispersion (Zhang, 2006), book-to-market (Asness, 1997), price (Bandarchuk and Hilscher, 2013), illiquidity (Amihud, 2002), capital gains (Grinblatt and Han, 2005), information diffusion (Da et al., 2014), failure probability (Avramov et al., 2007; Campbell et al., 2008), maximum daily return (Jacobs et al., 2016), equity duration (Dechow et al., 2004; Jiang et al., 2005), 52-week high price (George and Hwang, 2004), asset growth (Cooper et al., 2008), costs of goods sold (Sagi and Seasholes, 2007), and revenue volatility (Sagi and Seasholes, 2007). Measurement details of our chosen set of characteristics follow the reference papers and are described in Table 2.2.

Most of these characteristics are expected to have the same impact on momentum profits for the long portfolio (recent winners) and the short portfolio (recent losers). For instance, we expect a stronger momentum trend for smaller firms, irrespective of whether they are recent winners or recent losers. However, for some characteristics the relation to momentum profits depends on whether we consider the long portfolio or the short portfolio. For instance, according to Grinblatt and Han (2005) low capital gains losers as well as high capital gains winners are likely to yield stronger momentum returns. Opposed to this, low capital gains winners and high capital gains losers are expected to generate lower momentum returns. The expected influence of capital gains is thus different for the long and the short side.

Therefore, with reference to the characteristics capital gains, maximum daily return, and 52-week high price, we adjust variables in the following way:[9]

$$char_{new} = (char_{ordinary} - median_{char}) \cdot sign(R_{t-6,t-1} - R_{median,t-6,t-1}) \qquad (2.1)$$

The adjusted variables reverse the ranking for stocks which are part of the short side of the momentum portfolio, i.e. have a six-months return below the median. For instance, the expected influence of the adjusted variable capital gains is now positive for the long and short side of the momentum portfolio. This adjustment simplifies the structure of our tables

---

[9]The variable *information diffusion* is already adjusted in a similar manner by Da et al. (2014) and hence not included in this list.

and is necessary to conduct cross-sectional regressions of momentum profits on enhancing variables in the spirit of Bandarchuk and Hilscher (2013).

In line with respective reference studies in Table 2.2, we expect an inverse relationship between momentum and the following characteristics: size, r-squared, age, analyst coverage, book-to-market, price, information diffusion, and maximum daily return. To ease interpretations, we sort stocks in descending order according to these characteristics. That means, we always (double-) sort our stocks into portfolios such that long-short momentum returns should be highest in tertile 3 and lowest in tertile 1, if our initial expectations are met.

2.3.2.2 Methodological Setup

Given the fragmentation and disparity in the enhanced momentum literature, our study aims to take a comprehensive perspective on how stock characteristics relate to momentum returns. A central aspect within our study thus is combining the information of a variety of firm-specific attributes within a single metric. As emphasized, we refer to this metric as composite momentum enhancer.

We construct our composite momentum enhancer following procedures described by Lewellen (2015) and Green et al. (2017). Within these studies, authors have applied Fama-MacBeth regressions to forecast stock returns by combining various firm characteristics. To the best of our knowledge, our study is the first to apply a similar technique within the momentum literature.

In this regard, momentum profits are measured following Bandarchuk and Hilscher (2013), i.e. relative to whether or not a firm is able to outperform other stocks. Winner stocks are stocks having above-median returns. Loser stocks are stocks having below-median returns. Both, a stock's past and a stock's forward return are measured relative to respective medians. Accordingly, momentum profit is measured as a stock's forward return in relation to the median of all stock's forward returns, multiplied by a dummy variable, indicating whether the stock was a winner in the past six month (1) or a loser (-1):

$$R_{mom,t+1} = (R_{t+1} - R_{median,t+1}) \cdot sign(R_{t-6,t-1} - R_{median,t-6,t-1}) \qquad (2.2)$$

By doing so, stocks exhibiting negative signs in both, past and forward periods, yield positive momentum profits.

We construct our composite momentum enhancer as follows. Each month, for each country, we divide each of the eighteen characteristics into tertiles. For our internationally pooled sample, characteristics tertiles are calculated transnationally on a monthly basis. Each month for each country, we then run multivariate regressions of momentum profits on all eighteen characteristics tertiles simultaneously. On a five-year rolling basis, we apply averages of obtained regression coefficients for each of our eighteen characteristics tertiles as well as the corresponding constant and thus predict momentum profits for the next month solely upon the basis of our chosen set of characteristics. By applying average regression coefficients and constants of the most recent 60 months, we predict momentum profits for the following investment period - exclusively upon the basis of our eighteen stock characteristics.

2.3.3   Extreme Past Returns and Idiosyncratic Volatility

To rule out the possibility that our results are (exclusively) driven by potential interdependencies between recent winners, firm characteristics, and idiosyncratic volatility, we include two additional control variables within our study as in the spirit of Bandarchuk and Hilscher (2013). We do so by firstly measuring past returns in a direct way: Each month t, we calculate a stock's momentum strength in the following way:

$$Mom\_strength_{i,t} = exp(|r_{i,t-6,t-1} - r_{median,t-6,t-1}|) - 1 \qquad (2.3)$$

In equation (1), a stock's cumulative return over the past six months is denoted as log return. We subtract the country's median stock return from individual stock returns and take the absolute value. Following this approach, momentum strength indicates the extent to which past returns are extreme, i.e. both extreme losers as well as extreme winners have a higher momentum strength (Bandarchuk and Hilscher, 2013).

Besides extreme past returns, we account for firm-specific volatility. Idiosyncratic volatility is measured using regression residuals of ordinary monthly returns over the previous twelve months on the market factor (CAPM). Market returns indicate monthly excess returns on the market. We use the country-specific MSCI index as market reference and the one-month U.S. treasury bill rate as proxy for the risk-free rate.

2.4 Empirical Results

2.4.1 Portfolio Returns of Single Momentum-Enhancing Trading Strategies

We start by demonstrating that double-sorting stocks on characteristics and past returns leads to enhanced momentum profits and thus that characteristics have the potential to function as momentum enhancers within international equity markets. We do so by applying dependent and equally-weighted sorting techniques. In this section, we use "ordinary" double-sorts, which means we neither control for momentum strength and idiosyncratic volatility nor apply our composite-momentum metric.

At the end of each month, for each country we sort each characteristic into tertiles. Within each characteristic tertile, we calculate ordinary momentum strategies. This means we go long the tertile of past return (t-6,t-1) winners and short the tertile of past return (t-6,t-1) losers (P3-P1). We then calculate the differences between momentum returns of highest and lowest characteristics tertiles. With regard to size, r-squared, age, analyst coverage, book-to-market, price, information diffusion, and maximum daily return, we sort stocks in descending order because these stocks are supposed to weaken momentum profits as described above. For every characteristic, this procedure ensures highest (lowest) expected momentum returns in tertile 3 (1). Table 2.3 summarizes monthly returns obtained from ordinary double-sorts for each country-characteristic combination respectively.

Table 2.3: Unconditional Returns of Enhanced Momentum Strategies

This table reports average monthly returns obtained from ordinary double-sorts on IVOL, momentum strength, or characteristics (first-sort) and on past returns (second-sort). At the end of each month, for each country we sort each characteristic into tertiles. Within each characteristic tertile, we calculate ordinary momentum strategies. That is, we go long the tertile of past return (t-6,t-1) winners and short the tertile of past return (t-6,t-1) losers (P3-P1). We then calculate the differences between momentum returns of highest and the lowest characteristics tertiles. For IVOL, turnover, forecast dispersion, illiquidity, capital gains, failure probability, equity duration, 52-week high price, asset growth, costs of goods sold, and revenue volatility ascending order (Q3-Q1) is used. For size, r-squared, age, analyst coverage, book-to-market, price, information diffusion, and maximum daily return, stocks are sorted in descending order (Q1-Q3). The sample runs from M1:1989 to M6:2019. *, **, and *** indicate statistical significance at the 10%, 5%, and 1% level.

| | Panel A: North America, Japan, Pacific | | | | | | |
| | North America | | Japan | Pacific | | | |
	can	usa		atl	nzl	hkg	sin
IVOL	1.36%***	1.04%***	0.24%	1.65%***	0.63%	0.53%	0.16%
	(4.16)	(4.61)	(1.43)	(4.94)	(0.89)	(1.39)	(0.43)
mom_str	1.43%***	0.90%***	0.05%	1.88%***	1.63%**	0.47%	0.44%
	(4.07)	(2.75)	(0.18)	(5.25)	(2.62)	(1.11)	(1.14)
size	0.97%***	0.52%***	-0.12%	1.39%***	0.99%**	0.21%	0.43%
	(3.88)	(3.12)	(-0.73)	(4.47)	(2.10)	(0.59)	(1.24)
R^2	0.41%	0.37%**	0.35%**	1.27%***	1.31%**	0.89%**	1.06%***
	(1.59)	(2.09)	(2.54)	(4.42)	(2.39)	(2.45)	(2.97)
turn	-0.03%	0.51%**	-0.09%	-0.84%***	0.69%	-0.10%	-0.41%
	(-0.10)	(2.14)	(-0.40)	(-2.89)	(1.21)	(-0.26)	(-1.02)
age	0.90%***	1.03%***	0.71%*	1.46%***	-0.08%	0.75%*	0.89%**
	(3.02)	(4.32)	(1.82)	(5.09)	(-0.12)	(1.93)	(2.50)
nanalyst	0.75%***	0.40%**	0.03%	1.34%***	-0.15%	-0.23%	0.27%
	(2.80)	(2.48)	(0.18)	(4.70)	(-0.27)	(-0.69)	(0.72)
eps-disp	0.66%**	0.43%**	-0.02%	1.09%***	0.49%	0.72%**	-0.55%
	(2.08)	(2.19)	(-0.17)	(3.36)	(0.81)	(2.26)	(-1.57)
bm	0.88%***	0.72%***	0.74%***	0.49%	-0.29%	0.39%	0.87%**
	(2.78)	(3.12)	(4.48)	(1.38)	(-0.47)	(1.06)	(2.62)
price	0.94%***	0.28%	-0.80%***	0.42%	-0.11%	(0.00)	0.18%
	(3.17)	(1.28)	(-4.50)	(1.39)	(-0.21)	(0.37)	(0.56)
amihud	0.56%**	0.20%	0.15%	1.26%***	0.70%	0.42%	1.06%***
	(2.12)	(1.05)	(0.70)	(4.18)	(1.09)	(1.20)	(2.67)
cgs	0.78%*	-0.12%	-0.26%	0.75%**	0.97%*	0.82%*	0.11%
	(1.90)	(-0.29)	(-0.86)	(2.16)	(1.65)	(1.85)	(0.27)
ID	0.84%***	0.06%	0.04%	0.94%***	0.33%	1.15%***	-0.42%
	(2.72)	(0.24)	(0.23)	(3.30)	(0.52)	(3.35)	(-1.24)
failure	0.53%	0.45%**	-0.37%**	0.34%	-1.18%*	0.35%	-0.38%
	(1.62)	(2.06)	(-2.43)	(1.11)	(-1.72)	(0.77)	(-0.86)
max-ret	0.39%	0.73%*	0.76%**	0.02%	0.61%	1.08%**	-0.04%
	(1.16)	(1.66)	(2.62)	(0.07)	(1.12)	(2.18)	(-0.11)
dur	0.80%***	1.09%***	0.27%**	0.73%**	-0.92%	0.59%*	0.46%
	(2.93)	(4.75)	(2.00)	(2.65)	(-1.36)	(1.82)	(1.34)
p52-wh	1.24%***	0.12%	-0.06%	1.33%***	1.53%***	1.53%***	0.34%
	(3.18)	(0.24)	(-0.14)	(3.86)	(2.96)	(2.68)	(0.81)
ag	0.69%***	0.38%**	0.72%***	1.22%***	0.70%	0.46%	0.41%
	(2.83)	(2.38)	(5.66)	(4.29)	(1.12)	(1.35)	(1.28)
cogs	-0.20%	-0.21%	-0.23%*	0.17%	1.25%**	1.06%***	1.44%***
	(-0.70)	(-1.07)	(-1.87)	(0.59)	(2.14)	(2.94)	(3.78)
rev-vola	0.43%	0.37%***	0.38%***	0.15%	-0.08%	-0.27%	-0.31%
	(1.56)	(3.00)	(3.34)	(0.58)	(-0.14)	(-0.88)	(-0.87)
# t-stat>+2	13	13	6	13	5	6	5

Table 2.3 (Cont'd)

							Panel B: Europe					
	bel	den	fin	fra	ger	ita	net	nor	spa	swe	swi	uni
IVOL	1.61%*** (2.84)	0.53% (1.20)	-0.30% (-0.62)	0.42% (1.37)	1.15%*** (3.49)	0.85%** (2.46)	0.98%** (2.51)	1.08%** (2.05)	0.70%* (1.81)	0.74%* (1.90)	0.61%** (2.46)	1.18%*** (4.81)
mom_str	2.03%*** (3.58)	1.35%*** (3.20)	0.36% (0.63)	0.98%*** (2.82)	1.30%*** (3.68)	0.74%* (1.87)	0.99%** (2.42)	1.66%*** (3.10)	0.96%** (2.34)	0.38% (0.78)	0.96%*** (3.30)	1.38%*** (4.61)
size	1.14%** (2.40)	0.57% (1.33)	0.16% (0.32)	0.62%** (2.72)	0.46% (1.60)	0.18% (0.61)	1.31%*** (3.97)	0.56% (1.11)	0.56% (1.45)	0.48% (1.22)	0.53%** (2.15)	0.84%*** (4.46)
R^2	1.18%** (2.62)	0.68% (1.51)	0.48% (0.92)	0.32% (1.18)	-0.06% (-0.18)	0.48% (1.61)	0.86%** (2.58)	1.25%** (2.19)	0.38% (1.05)	0.44% (1.12)	0.91%*** (3.66)	1.14%*** (5.69)
turn	0.08% (0.16)	-0.05% (-0.11)	0.11% (0.20)	-0.14% (-0.39)	0.36% (1.15)	0.42% (1.22)	-0.27% (-0.70)	0.02% (0.04)	0.18% (0.49)	-0.42% (-0.98)	-0.11% (-0.40)	-0.45%** (-2.26)
age	1.59%*** (3.46)	1.06%* (1.89)	0.43% (0.79)	0.59%** (2.25)	1.38%*** (4.44)	0.18% (0.53)	-0.88% (-0.97)	0.75% (1.45)	0.23% (0.49)	1.12%*** (2.80)	1.30%*** (4.39)	1.09%*** (3.74)
nanalyst	0.69% (1.49)	0.44% (1.12)	0.13% (0.26)	0.29% (1.16)	-0.30% (-0.98)	0.29% (1.15)	0.87%** (2.37)	0.59% (1.14)	0.82%** (2.28)	1.01%** (2.57)	0.79%*** (2.97)	1.16%*** (5.30)
eps-disp	1.27%** (2.12)	-0.23% (-0.52)	-0.33% (-0.69)	0.39% (1.36)	-0.13% (-0.38)	-0.12% (-0.36)	0.95%** (2.41)	0.74% (1.53)	0.49% (1.33)	-0.24% (-0.56)	-0.05% (-0.19)	0.53%** (2.46)
bm	0.89% (1.62)	1.07%** (2.29)	0.05% (0.11)	0.35% (1.25)	0.92%*** (3.29)	0.55%* (1.85)	0.78%** (2.16)	0.67% (1.21)	0.08% (0.22)	1.38%*** (3.47)	0.85%*** (3.57)	0.85%*** (3.81)
price	0.90%* (1.81)	0.03% (0.06)	0.52% (1.08)	-0.04% (-0.13)	0.59%* (1.71)	-0.12% (-0.39)	0.35% (0.91)	0.83% (1.53)	0.22% (0.59)	-0.59% (-1.38)	0.49%* (1.80)	0.51%** (2.56)
amihud	0.58% (1.06)	0.29% (0.64)	0.04% (0.07)	0.47% (1.55)	-1.15% (-1.23)	-0.21% (-0.51)	1.00%*** (2.82)	0.19% (0.33)	0.10% (0.25)	0.51% (1.36)	0.77%*** (2.73)	1.02%*** (2.80)
cgs	0.62% (1.03)	-0.20% (-0.38)	-0.01% (-0.01)	0.22% (0.58)	1.35%** (2.05)	1.26%*** (2.86)	1.35%*** (3.02)	1.45%** (2.37)	0.78%* (1.72)	0.52% (1.03)	0.40% (1.31)	0.77%** (2.29)
ID	0.07% (0.13)	0.22% (0.50)	-0.04% (-0.07)	0.20% (0.75)	1.01%*** (3.14)	0.04% (0.12)	0.36% (0.89)	0.63% (1.22)	0.37% (0.91)	0.31% (0.76)	0.19% (0.80)	0.43%* (1.95)
failure	0.93%** (1.98)	-0.77% (-1.50)	0.69% (1.23)	-0.28% (-0.85)	0.08% (0.23)	0.04% (0.11)	0.50% (1.29)	1.04%* (1.87)	0.40% (0.96)	0.18% (0.45)	0.70%** (2.50)	0.18% (0.81)
max-ret	0.92% (1.59)	-0.18% (-0.37)	0.00% (-0.01)	1.04%*** (3.01)	1.09%** (2.57)	0.70%* (1.93)	0.75%* (1.72)	0.77% (1.27)	0.33% (0.79)	1.23%*** (2.67)	0.55% (1.63)	0.01% (0.03)
dur	1.38%*** (2.70)	-0.18% (-0.39)	1.18%** (2.35)	0.49% (1.59)	0.54% (1.62)	0.50%* (1.72)	0.82%** (2.20)	1.51%*** (3.07)	-0.17% (-0.49)	1.16%*** (2.79)	0.96%*** (3.70)	0.91%*** (4.02)
p52-wh	1.47%** (2.27)	1.51%*** (3.15)	0.13% (0.19)	0.03% (0.06)	1.20%*** (2.63)	0.71% (1.54)	1.07%** (2.12)	1.44%** (2.11)	1.46%*** (2.80)	0.30% (0.63)	0.74%* (1.89)	1.35%*** (3.91)
ag	0.55% (0.99)	0.46% (0.96)	0.72% (1.42)	0.65%** (2.44)	0.73%** (2.55)	0.10% (0.35)	0.36% (1.00)	1.02%* (1.91)	0.89%** (2.49)	1.32%*** (3.23)	0.41%* (1.71)	0.75%*** (4.02)
cogs	0.11% (0.21)	-0.65% (-1.23)	-0.72% (-1.41)	0.44%* (1.97)	-0.23% (-0.75)	-0.59%* (-1.89)	-0.65%* (-1.74)	-0.13% (-0.22)	-0.41% (-1.10)	0.11% (0.28)	-0.07% (-0.25)	-0.14% (-0.66)
rev-vola	0.40% (0.80)	0.31% (0.64)	0.68% (1.30)	0.12% (0.55)	0.32% (1.11)	0.06% (0.21)	0.42% (1.03)	-0.01% (-0.02)	0.04% (0.09)	0.67%* (1.69)	-0.23% (-0.89)	0.69%*** (3.34)
# t-stat>+2	8	3	1	5	9	2	11	6	4	6	10	15

Table 2.3 (Cont'd)

	bra	chi	chn	gre	ind	ido	mal	mex	pak	phi	pol	soa	sok	tai	tha	tur
Panel C: Emerging Markets																
IVOL	0.04% (0.06)	1.03% (1.55)	0.50%* (1.76)	-0.60% (-0.72)	0.46% (1.09)	-0.91% (-0.94)	-0.43% (-1.28)	0.27% (0.54)	-0.04% (-0.05)	0.07% (0.11)	0.73% (1.32)	1.04%** (2.49)	0.50% (1.07)	0.88%** (2.53)	-0.62% (-1.18)	-0.50% (-0.89)
mom_str	-1.02% (-1.37)	0.71% (1.31)	-0.03% (-0.08)	0.68% (0.78)	0.89%** (2.02)	0.09% (0.10)	-0.03% (-0.07)	1.09%** (1.97)	0.38% (0.43)	-0.67% (-0.77)	1.43%** (2.30)	1.92%*** (4.51)	-0.28% (-1.07)	0.80%* (1.93)	0.12% (0.19)	-0.17% (-0.27)
size	0.68% (1.06)	0.13% (0.24)	0.05% (0.14)	-0.54% (-0.76)	0.44% (1.12)	0.81% (1.10)	-0.23% (-0.67)	0.60% (1.15)	-0.91% (-0.96)	0.16% (0.23)	0.34% (0.60)	0.39% (1.08)	0.59% (1.22)	-0.15% (-0.44)	-0.81% (-1.05)	1.17%* (1.71)
R^2	0.61% (0.92)	0.02% (0.04)	-0.48% (-1.45)	1.70%** (2.07)	0.32% (0.83)	-2.21% (-2.38)	0.89%** (2.50)	0.15% (0.29)	0.73% (0.78)	0.30% (0.39)	0.59% (1.01)	1.53%*** (3.46)	-0.26% (-0.59)	0.75%** (2.52)	0.35% (0.61)	-0.81% (-1.26)
turn	1.20%* (1.92)	0.55% (0.91)	0.69%** (1.99)	-0.50% (-0.56)	0.06% (0.14)	2.12%** (2.07)	-0.96%** (-2.55)	0.46% (0.92)	-1.02% (-1.10)	-1.31%* (-1.73)	-0.08% (-0.12)	-0.33% (-0.81)	0.43% (1.00)	1.16%*** (3.50)	-0.41% (-0.64)	0.00% (0.00)
age	1.54%*** (2.63)	0.21% (0.22)	0.68%** (2.19)	0.39% (0.54)	-0.32% (-0.99)	0.11% (0.14)	0.58%* (1.67)	0.46% (0.95)	-0.77% (-0.61)	-1.38%* (-1.65)	-0.09% (-0.15)	0.94%** (2.28)	0.23% (0.58)	0.52% (1.50)	0.00% (-0.01)	-0.06% (-0.09)
nanalyst	0.27% (0.40)	-0.17% (-0.33)	-0.68% (-1.48)	-0.34% (-0.39)	0.46% (1.31)	-1.51%* (-1.69)	-0.31% (-0.79)	0.51% (1.07)	0.10% (0.14)	0.01% (0.01)	0.44% (0.80)	0.47% (1.14)	-0.06% (-0.14)	-0.27% (-0.92)	-0.18% (-0.31)	-0.19% (-0.31)
eps-disp	0.95% (1.11)	0.84% (1.45)	0.75% (1.02)	-0.48% (-0.52)	0.52% (1.18)	-0.32% (-0.40)	-0.77%** (-2.07)	0.74% (1.26)	-0.28% (-0.34)	0.15% (0.23)	1.52%** (2.31)	0.58% (1.39)	0.84%* (1.91)	-0.29% (-0.81)	-0.05% (-0.09)	1.02% (1.55)
bm	1.00% (1.47)	-0.51% (-1.21)	-0.32% (-0.99)	1.05% (1.13)	1.41%*** (3.46)	-1.14% (-1.06)	1.08%*** (3.21)	0.99%** (1.99)	0.04% (0.04)	-0.01% (-0.01)	-0.33% (-0.55)	0.48% (1.35)	0.00% (0.00)	0.96%*** (2.58)	1.08%* (1.66)	-0.28% (-0.47)
price	-0.74% (-1.13)	-0.16% (-0.29)	-0.71%* (-1.80)	-1.11% (-1.46)	-1.11%** (-2.58)	-1.14% (-1.31)	-0.81%** (-2.02)	0.49% (1.04)	-0.96% (-1.15)	-0.81% (-1.04)	-0.04% (-0.06)	0.59% (1.38)	0.09% (0.20)	-1.22%*** (-3.32)	-0.11% (-0.19)	-0.10% (-0.15)
amihud	0.00% (0.00)	0.10% (0.19)	-0.06% (-0.16)	0.93% (1.01)	0.80%** (2.08)	-0.87% (-0.96)	0.56%* (1.71)	-0.17% (-0.31)	0.41% (0.43)	1.26%* (1.65)	-0.47% (-0.65)	0.30% (0.71)	-0.36% (-0.73)	-0.24% (-0.71)	-0.49% (-0.80)	1.03% (1.46)
cgs	0.97% (1.27)	0.36% (0.70)	-1.59%*** (-2.79)	1.07% (1.05)	1.12%** (2.20)	0.12% (0.12)	-0.37% (-0.95)	-0.01% (-0.02)	-0.33% (-0.40)	-0.18% (-0.21)	0.21% (0.32)	0.35% (0.75)	0.40% (0.71)	1.33%*** (2.72)	1.84%*** (3.00)	-0.71% (-1.08)
ID	1.45%** (2.19)	0.40% (0.90)	-0.17% (-0.48)	0.07% (0.09)	0.98%** (2.41)	0.71% (0.74)	-0.13% (-0.32)	0.00% (0.00)	2.54%*** (3.09)	0.70% (1.00)	1.49%** (2.51)	0.82%** (2.23)	0.01% (0.01)	0.90%*** (2.67)	-0.29% (-0.52)	0.75% (1.00)
failure	0.31% (0.41)	0.43% (0.82)	-0.39% (-1.06)	0.35% (0.50)	-0.66% (-1.48)	-1.15% (-0.95)	-0.59% (-1.39)	0.07% (0.13)	0.12% (0.10)	0.28% (0.21)	0.50% (0.59)	0.55% (1.28)	0.12% (0.32)	-0.10% (-0.26)	-0.40% (-0.57)	-0.90% (-1.53)
max-ret	-1.54%** (-2.23)	-0.48% (-0.80)	1.69%*** (3.82)	1.83%** (2.30)	0.66% (1.48)	0.29% (0.27)	0.34% (0.79)	-0.63% (-1.01)	-1.46% (-1.57)	1.70%** (2.21)	0.27% (0.44)	0.48% (1.12)	0.61% (1.40)	0.61% (1.39)	-0.36% (-0.64)	1.10% (1.63)
dur	-0.59% (-0.91)	0.00% (0.00)	-0.54%* (-1.85)	0.57% (0.65)	0.65% (1.59)	-1.46% (-1.48)	-0.03% (-0.11)	-0.11% (-0.22)	-0.05% (-0.06)	-0.72% (-1.03)	0.87% (1.37)	0.37% (0.96)	0.79%* (1.92)	-0.02% (-0.09)	0.60% (1.29)	-0.36% (-0.69)
p52-wh	-1.72%** (-2.11)	0.16% (0.27)	-0.92%* (-1.78)	0.82% (0.83)	1.08%** (2.22)	1.31% (1.35)	0.40% (0.81)	-0.49% (-0.76)	1.33%* (1.66)	0.18% (0.21)	0.70% (1.10)	0.91%* (1.91)	0.22% (0.34)	1.14%** (2.16)	1.30% (1.63)	0.15% (0.21)
ag	0.37% (0.57)	-0.60% (-1.06)	0.63%** (2.33)	0.62% (0.83)	0.49% (1.15)	0.22% (0.29)	-0.27% (-0.72)	-0.06% (-0.11)	-0.90% (-0.98)	0.13% (0.21)	0.66% (1.12)	0.21% (0.56)	0.07% (0.18)	0.95%*** (2.90)	-0.18% (-0.32)	-0.61% (-1.02)
cogs	0.67% (0.98)	0.19% (0.36)	0.13% (0.46)	0.96% (1.58)	0.43% (1.24)	0.29% (0.43)	0.87%*** (2.68)	-0.75% (-1.49)	0.26% (0.30)	0.22% (0.24)	-0.60% (-0.83)	1.00%** (2.34)	0.84%* (1.75)	0.82%** (2.51)	0.44% (0.78)	1.43%** (2.20)
rev-vola	1.00% (1.29)	-0.69% (-1.63)	-0.05% (-0.11)	-1.27% (-1.58)	0.31% (0.69)	1.85%* (1.73)	0.15% (0.41)	0.53% (0.97)	0.49% (0.50)	0.07% (0.09)	0.50% (0.83)	0.33% (0.73)	0.19% (0.49)	-0.10% (-0.36)	-0.08% (-0.16)	1.49%** (2.30)
# t-stat>|2|	2	0	3	2	6	1	3	0	1	1	3	6	0	9	1	2

As shown in Table 2.3, double-sorting on characteristics and past returns best functions within the United Kingdom, being followed by Australia, Canada, the United States, Netherlands, and Switzerland.[10] On the other hand, the profitability of enhancing strategies deviates for Asian countries. In Japan, for instance, double-sorting on price and past returns leads to a statistically significant monthly negative return of 0.80% (t-statistics of -4.50). This finding implies that the characteristic *price* has a reversed effect within Japan, yet is per se significant in enhancing momentum returns when applying ascending rather than descending sorting technique (Q3-Q1). Within other Asian countries, though, enhancing strategies neither work in both directions, i.e. they neither yield statistically significant positive nor negative returns. This for instance holds for South Korea, Pakistan, the Philippines or Thailand. This finding is in line with existing literature stating that within Asian countries ordinary momentum strategies do not tend to perform well either (Griffin et al., 2003; Chui et al., 2010). Few characteristics occasionally, though, seem to matter even across multiple Asian countries. In Japan, Hong Kong, Malaysia, Singapore, and Taiwan, for instance, R^2 matters strongly (t-statistics greater than two). In a similar vein, we find a strong segmentation within European countries. Whereas double-sortings perform well within United Kingdom, Netherlands, Switzerland, Belgium, and Germany, they hardly function within Denmark, Finland or Italy.

Highest returns on average are obtained when double-sorting on momentum strength (average monthly excess return of 0.74%), 52-week high price (0.69%) as well as r-squared (0.51%), book-to-market (0.51%), and age (0.51%). In line with Bandarchuk and Hilscher (2013), idiosyncratic volatility also appears to be an important momentum enhancer with an average return of 0.50% per month across all countries. Lowest mean returns result from double-sorts on price (-0.09%), turnover (0.04%), and failure probability (0.06%).

On an aggregate basis, we find particularly the characteristics momentum strength (sixteen out of thirty-five countries), r-squared (fifteen out of thirty-five), age (thirteen out of thirty-five), book-to-market (thirteen out of thirty-five), as well as 52-week high price (thirteen out of thirty-five) to lead to statistically highly significant enhanced momentum returns

---

[10]This inference is drawn by the absolute number of characteristics yielding monthly positive enhanced returns with t-statistics greater than two.

(t-statistic greater than two).

In total, our results obtained from dependent double-sorting techniques provide first evidence for the ability of characteristics to function as momentum enhancers in a global data set. Our findings, however, also imply a high variability of the importance of characteristics across countries.

Overall, average returns obtained from double-sortings are highest for Belgium (0.92%), Australia (0.85%), Norway (0.80%), Canada (0.72%), and United Kingdom (0.71%). Average double-sorts within the U.S. amount to 0.46%. These findings are roughly consistent with returns obtained from classical momentum strategies which also tend to be highest for Australia (1.16%) and Belgium (1.15%). An exception remains Brazil, for which we obtain ordinary momentum returns of 1.19%, while average enhanced momentum returns within Brazil amount to 0.27%. Within the U.S., classical monthly momentum returns amount to comparable 0.34%. Accordingly, countries exhibiting lowest ordinary momentum returns are also among the ones with lowest average enhanced momentum returns (e.g. China).

2.4.2   Fama-MacBeth Regressions of Composite Momentum

Our baseline analyses start by testing which portion of actual momentum profits can be explained by predicted momentum. The rationale beyond is that if stock characteristics have no power in explaining momentum profits, their ability to forecast momentum profits should be close to zero, at least once controlling for idiosyncratic volatility and extreme past returns.

To interact ordinary momentum with predicted momentum, we run univariate Fama-MacBeth regressions of actual momentum profits on predicted momentum profit tertiles. As a next step, we control for actual momentum strength tertiles and IVOL tertiles (multivariate Fama-MacBeth regressions) to account for potential interdependencies highlighted by Bandarchuk and Hilscher (2013). Table 2.4 summarizes respective outcomes on a country-basis as well as for our internationally pooled data set.

Table 2.4: Fama-MacBeth Regressions on
Predicted Momentum Profits

This table reports Fama-MacBeth regressions of actual momentum profits on predicted momentum profit tertiles only (univariate) as well as on predicted momentum profit tertiles, actual momentum strength tertiles. and actual IVOL tertiles (multivariate) on a country-basis as well as for our internationally pooled sample. The internationally pooled sample contains all countries apart from the U.S. market. Predicted momentum profits are calculated using country-specific predictors. For this purpose, each month for each country, we divide each of the eighteen characteristics into tertiles. For our internationally pooled sample, characteristics tertiles are calculated transnationally on a monthly basis. Each month for each country, we then run ordinary regressions of momentum profits on all eighteen characteristics tertiles simultaneously (multivariate). Then, on a five-year rolling basis, we apply average regression coefficients and constants for each of our eighteen characteristics tertiles and predict momentum profits for the next month solely upon the basis of our chosen set of characteristics. As a next step, we test how well our predicted momentum measure is in explaining actual momentum profits. That is, we run Fama-MacBeth regressions of actual momentum profits on predicted momentum profits tertiles (univariate) as well as on predicted momentum profits tertiles, actual momentum strength deciles, and actual IVOL tertiles (multivariate). For illustration purposes, all coefficients are multiplied by 100. The sample runs from M1:1989 to M6:2019. Respective t-statistics are indicated within parentheses. *, **, and *** indicate statistical significance at the 10%, 5%, and 1% level.

	Panel A: Univariate	Panel B: Multivariate		
Country	Predicted Mom	Predicted Mom	Mom-Str	IVOL
atl	0.8982***	0.7886***	0.2867***	0.0176
	(10.43)	(9.30)	(3.57)	(0.25)
bel	0.2655***	0.2243***	0.3887***	-0.0991
	(2.84)	(2.38)	(3.17)	(-0.94)
bra	0.3802**	0.3279**	0.2190	0.1457
	(2.40)	(2.17)	(1.33)	(1.01)
can	0.9835***	0.9066***	0.2268***	-0.0574
	(12.00)	(10.28)	(2.67)	(-0.78)
chi	0.1506	0.1374	0.2332*	0.0770
	(1.25)	(1.19)	(1.70)	(0.53)
chn	0.4013***	0.2561***	0.0655	0.1947***
	(4.07)	(3.12)	(0.78)	(3.47)
den	0.2944***	0.2297**	0.3696***	-0.0180
	(2.71)	(2.02)	(3.40)	(-0.17)
fin	0.0426	0.0278	0.0012	0.0026
	(0.41)	(0.27)	(0.01)	(0.03)
fra	0.3008***	0.2720***	0.2925***	-0.0187
	(3.46)	(4.30)	(3.40)	(-0.33)
ger	0.4847***	0.3480***	0.3391***	0.0187
	(4.34)	(4.08)	(3.83)	(0.27)
gre	0.6000**	0.5933***	0.3178	-0.1370
	(2.43)	(2.80)	(1.29)	(-0.81)
hkg	0.6435***	0.5957***	0.2260**	0.1087
	(5.84)	(5.42)	(2.02)	(1.23)
ido	0.3117	0.3805*	0.2693	-0.2013
	(1.36)	(1.66)	(1.41)	(-1.04)
ind	0.8491***	0.6812***	0.2483**	0.3076***
	(5.94)	(5.10)	(2.20)	(3.08)
ita	0.2885***	0.2273***	0.2602***	0.1148
	(3.62)	(3.15)	(2.93)	(1.38)
jap	0.2848***	0.2977***	0.0756	0.0272
	(4.78)	(5.32)	(1.13)	(0.82)

Table 2.4 (Cont'd): Fama-MacBeth Regressions
on Predicted Momentum Profits

Country	Panel A: Univariate	Panel B: Multivariate		
	Predicted Mom	Predicted Mom	Mom-Str	IVOL
mal	0.5414***	0.4978***	0.1324	-0.0685
	(5.03)	(4.95)	(1.19)	(-0.90)
mex	0.3083**	0.2781**	0.3893**	-0.0665
	(2.26)	(2.14)	(2.63)	(-0.68)
net	0.3015***	0.2052**	0.3153***	0.0869
	(3.27)	(2.39)	(3.25)	(1.03)
nor	0.3421***	0.3250**	0.4592***	-0.0002
	(2.83)	(2.62)	(3.39)	(0.00)
nzl	0.4604***	0.4301***	0.3891***	0.0249
	(3.45)	(3.32)	(3.26)	(0.19)
pak	0.3536*	0.1070	0.6619***	0.1321
	(1.71)	(0.56)	(3.33)	(0.66)
phi	0.2229	0.1607	0.2479	0.0904
	(1.46)	(1.04)	(1.45)	(0.52)
pol	0.1409	0.0487	0.3015**	0.0068
	(0.73)	(0.34)	(1.99)	(0.05)
sin	0.5891***	0.5570***	0.1244	-0.0709
	(5.70)	(5.47)	(1.18)	(-0.84)
soa	0.2215**	0.2168**	0.3681***	0.0554
	(2.34)	(2.29)	(3.95)	(0.68)
sok	0.5133***	0.3799***	0.1754	0.0883
	(4.44)	(3.46)	(1.39)	(0.84)
spa	0.1603*	0.1490*	0.2498***	0.1104
	(1.76)	(1.65)	(2.67)	(1.47)
swe	0.5774***	0.5917***	0.2488**	-0.0576
	(5.67)	(6.19)	(2.52)	(-0.71)
swi	0.3094***	0.2830***	0.2026***	0.1053*
	(4.50)	(4.50)	(2.98)	(1.81)
tai	0.4190***	0.4072***	0.1796*	-0.0596
	(4.19)	(4.32)	(1.83)	(-0.77)
tha	0.1679	0.3067	-0.1079	0.0892
	(0.88)	(1.64)	(-0.59)	(0.61)
tur	0.3398***	0.3759***	0.4125***	0.0695
	(2.90)	(3.25)	(2.90)	(0.47)
uni	0.6692***	0.6369***	0.2469***	-0.0320
	(9.25)	(9.19)	(3.35)	(-0.58)
usa	0.4448***	0.4254***	0.1363*	0.0248
	(6.31)	(7.95)	(1.70)	(0.58)
internat	0.5185***	0.4863***	0.2270***	0.0050
	(13.36)	(12.55)	(5.88)	(0.16)

As shown in Table 2.4, our composite momentum predictor is statistically significant (t-statistics greater than two) in explaining actual momentum profits within 27 out of 35 countries.[11] Within 23 out of these 27 countries, we obtain statistical significance at the 1%-level. Countries for which we obtain statistical significance at the 1%-level comprise Australia, Belgium, Canada, China, Denmark, France, Germany, Hong Kong, India, Italy, Japan, Malaysia, Netherlands, Norway, New Zealand, Singapore, South Korea, Sweden, Switzerland, Taiwan, Turkey, United Kingdom as well as United States.

Specifically, t-statistics are highest for Canada (12.00), Australia (10.43), and United Kingdom (9.25). Within the U.S., t-statistics are still considerable 6.31. For our internationally pooled sample (comprising all of our chosen countries with the exception of the U.S.), t-statistics amount to 13.36. Respective regression coefficients range from highest 0.98 (Canada) to lowest 0.04 (Finland). For the U.S., we report a regression coefficient of 0.44, for our internationally pooled sample the respective coefficient equals 0.52.

Once controlling for idiosyncratic volatility and momentum strength, predicted momentum remains statistically significant (t-statistics greater than two) within all out of the reported 27 countries as well as within the international sample, with t-statistics and regression coefficients being only slightly reduced. Beyond, we find statistical significances of our predicted momentum measure to slightly increase when accounting for extreme past returns and firm-specific volatility within France, Greece, Japan, Sweden, Taiwan, Turkey, and the United States. We interpret these findings to provide empirical evidence for a systematic link between characteristics and momentum profits that is not explained by idiosyncratic volatility or extreme past returns.

2.4.3   Composite-Enhanced Trading Strategy

In this section, we study returns of portfolios formed using our composite-momentum metric. We apply 3x3 double-sorts using firm-specific predicted momentum and cumulative past returns. That is, within each predicted momentum tertile, we calculate ordinary momentum

---

[11]Within Chile, Finland, Indonesia, Pakistan, Philippines, Poland, Spain as well as Thailand, univariate regressions of actual momentum profits on predicted momentum yield t-statistics smaller than two.

strategies, then taking differences between ordinary momentum returns of highest/lowest predicted momentum tertiles (Q3-Q1). Ordinary momentum returns are again calculated going long (short) the tertile of past return winners (losers). Excluding the most recent month, we use a six months period to calculate past returns and establish the momentum portfolios. We apply dependent and equally-weighted sorting techniques. Most importantly, given the applied sorting technique, this investment strategy becomes neutral to ordinary momentum strategies. It is thus less likely "to be based on any kind of risk story" (Hong et al., 2000, p. 284).

Table 2.5 summarizes monthly long-short returns on a country-basis. Additionally, we report descriptive statistics (skewness, kurtosis, minimum returns) for monthly returns obtained from double-sorts on our predicted momentum measure and past returns. Lastly, we regress respective returns on Carhart's[12] (1997) four factors and report corresponding exposure with regard to the momentum factor (Winner-Minus-Loser; WML) and regression alphas.

As illustrated, highest country returns are obtained for Switzerland (1.29%), Germany (1.12%), Norway (1.12%), Brazil (1.10%), and Belgium (1.07%). Conversely, we report lowest statistically significant returns for France (0.64%), United Kingdom (0.72%), Taiwan (0.73%), and Japan (0.87%). For the U.S. market we obtain monthly portfolio returns of 0.88% (t-statistics: 3.13). For our internationally pooled sample, we obtain monthly excess returns of 1.14% (t-statistics of 5.27). As exemplified, for these countries our results do not indicate higher skewness, kurtosis or minimum returns for composite-enhanced momentum returns than for ordinary momentum returns reported in Table 2.1. Conversely, we for instance obtain insignificant results among others for countries such as China, South Korea or Malaysia as well as small European countries as for instance Denmark or Finland. Notably, these countries are also among the countries for which single characteristics-enhanced momentum strategies work least as illustrated within Table 2.3.

---

[12]The Carhart (1997) 4-factor model extends the Fama-French 3-factor model by adding an additional factor accounting for momentum returns (WML) besides the market, size, and value factors.

Table 2.5: Return- and Risk-Characteristics
of Predicted Momentum Strategies

This table reports descriptive statistics (average monthly returns, skewness, kurtosis, minimum returns) of returns obtained from dependent double-sorts on predicted momentum profits and past returns on a country-basis. Predicted momentum profits are calculated using country-specific predictors. For this purpose, each month for each country, we divide each of the eighteen characteristics into deciles. Each month, for each country we then run ordinary regressions of momentum profits on all eighteen characteristics tertiles simultaneously (multivariate). Then, on a five-year rolling basis, we apply average regression coefficients and constants for each of our eighteen characteristics tertiles and predict momentum profits for the next month solely upon the basis of our chosen set of characteristics. As a next step, we regress returns obtained from double-sorts on predicted momentum profits and past returns on Carhart's four factors (SMB, HML, WML, and MKTRF). We report respective regression constants. The sample runs from M1:1989 to M6:2019. Corresponding t-statistics are indicated within parentheses. *, **, and *** indicate statistical significance at the 10%, 5%, and 1% level.

	Ret Diff	Skew	Kurt	Min	Constant	WML Beta
atl	1.00%***	-0.13	4.58	-21.07%	0.00883**	0.21910***
	(3.13)				(2.55)	(3.52)
bel	1.07%**	1.05	7.92	-14.60%	0.01233**	0.11543
	(2.12)				(2.38)	(1.15)
bra	1.10%*	0.26	4.08	-23.40%	0.01089*	-0.15063
	(1.82)				(1.74)	(-1.49)
can	0.97%***	0.14	7.33	-28.61%	0.00895***	0.11476**
	(2.94)				(2.69)	(2.35)
chi	0.51%	0.50	4.27	-18.97%	-0.00019	0.46283***
	(1.06)				(-0.04)	(3.32)
chn	0.38%	-0.71	6.25	-20.46%	0.00610**	-0.09267
	(1.36)				(2.24)	(-1.39)
den	0.03%	-0.05	4.78	-29.92%	-0.00433	0.29526***
	(0.05)				(-0.74)	(2.93)
fin	-0.17%	0.17	3.37	-18.58%	-0.00156	0.04291
	(-0.35)				(-0.31)	(0.46)
fra	0.64%*	-0.37	8.70	-30.34%	0.00298	0.46750***
	(1.86)				(0.92)	(7.06)
ger	1.12%***	-0.62	7.11	-28.09%	0.00740**	0.48057***
	(3.09)				(2.34)	(8.75)
gre	0.66%	-2.06	15.28	-93.60%	0.00255	0.48606***
	(0.71)				(0.26)	(3.51)
hkg	0.36%	-1.93	13.00	-56.84%	0.00354	0.30600***
	(0.75)				(0.78)	(4.07)
ind	0.77%	-0.10	6.55	-33.42%	0.00110	0.44080***
	(1.51)				(0.25)	(6.29)
ido	0.17%	1.36	18.15	-52.61%	-0.00215	0.03147
	(0.18)				(-0.23)	(0.25)
ita	0.38%	-0.12	6.43	-31.96%	0.00166	0.37421***
	(0.98)				(0.45)	(5.06)
jap	0.87%***	-0.13	5.29	-18.91%	0.00804***	0.18611***
	(3.31)				(3.29)	(3.43)

Table 2.5 (Cont'd):
Return- and Risk-Characteristics of
Predicted Momentum Strategies

	Ret Diff	Skew	Kurt	Min	Constant	WML Beta
mal	0.09%	0.96	13.22	-23.44%	0.00141	-0.16234***
	(0.24)				(0.37)	(-2.70)
mex	0.68%	-1.40	13.13	-48.57%	0.00567	0.31770**
	(1.22)				(0.92)	(2.37)
net	1.02%**	0.28	5.13	-30.55%	0.00628*	0.51654***
	(2.43)				(1.64)	(7.98)
nor	1.12%*	0.01	4.22	-28.87%	0.00793	0.19403**
	(1.91)				(1.31)	(2.15)
nzl	0.87%	0.51	4.25	-14.68%	0.00029	0.52660***
	(1.41)				(0.05)	(4.10)
pak	0.02%	0.25	5.07	-42.96%	-0.00192	0.07590
	(0.03)				(-0.20)	(0.40)
phi	-0.74%	1.42	11.86	-25.61%	-0.00776	0.09833
	(-1.07)				(-1.09)	(0.84)
pol	-0.75%	-0.31	3.13	-22.32%	-0.00832	0.15925
	(-1.29)				(-1.39)	(1.32)
sin	0.37%	1.07	9.47	-24.75%	0.00457	0.14156*
	(0.84)				(1.00)	(1.76)
soa	0.41%	-0.25	4.60	-24.07%	-0.00123	0.27332***
	(0.96)				(-0.27)	(3.32)
sok	0.59%	-1.15	13.24	-64.53%	0.00035	0.3759***
	(1.12)				(0.07)	(5.08)
spa	0.61%	-0.29	4.42	-31.37%	0.00485	0.16988*
	(1.43)				(1.07)	(1.95)
swe	0.94%**	0.43	5.02	-24.85%	0.00814**	0.21280***
	(2.31)				(2.02)	(3.56)
swi	1.29%***	-0.44	6.31	-24.92%	0.01087***	0.46046***
	(4.16)				(3.87)	(8.32)
tai	0.73%*	-0.30	5.96	-22.15%	0.00631*	0.40631***
	(1.76)				(1.67)	(5.03)
tha	0.95%	-0.72	13.24	-72.00%	0.00796	0.27114***
	(1.42)				(1.16)	(2.83)
tur	0.85%	0.36	4.08	-25.75%	0.00761	-0.01000
	(1.50)				(1.30)	(-0.08)
uni	0.72%***	0.09	9.49	-26.23%	0.00593**	0.18600***
	(2.72)				(2.33)	(3.83)
usa	0.88%***	0.26	6.57	-20.60%	0.00988***	0.34823***
	(3.13)				(4.22)	(8.10)
internat	1.14%***	-0.01	5.25	15.51%	0.00902***	0.27152***
	(5.27)				(3.88)	(3.62)

Correlation between ordinary momentum returns reported in Table 2.1 and composite-enhanced momentum returns shown in Table 2.5 amount to 0.54 within the U.S. market, while we observe a high variability for international markets. Highest correlations between ordinary and composite-enhanced momentum returns across international markets are observed within France (0.60), India (0.53) and Switzerland (0.53) as well as Germany (0.50). Conversely, hardly any correlations between ordinary and composite-enhanced momentum returns are observed within countries such as Finland, Thailand, and Turkey. These findings are again in line with results reported in Section 2.4.1 indicating that single-characteristics enhanced strategies neither seem to work within these countries. Also, when regressing reported composite-enhanced momentum returns on Carhart's four factors, a considerable and mostly significant alpha remains within almost all of the markets exhibiting statistically significant composite-enhanced momentum returns. Beyond, we report a statistically significant WML beta in these markets, providing evidence on a common root cause for ordinary and composite-enhanced momentum returns.

Still, on an aggregate basis, we interpret results obtained from our out-of-sample tests as a systematic pattern between stock characteristics and composite-enhanced momentum returns that is not captured by either idiosyncratic volatility, momentum strength, or multi-factor asset pricing models to its full extent.

2.5 Cross-Country Analyses: Determinants of (Composite-Enhanced) Momentum Returns

2.5.1 Country Characteristics

What explains global differences of composite-momentum returns reported in Section 2.4? In this section, we apply cross-country analyses to empirically analyze which theoretical momentum explanation best fits reported findings. In accordance with theoretical explanations of ordinary momentum returns outlined in Section 2.2 and prior academic cross-country studies, we identify four sets of country characteristics. Detailed country variable descriptions are provided in Appendix A.2 of the Electronic Supplementary Material. In the following, we summarize applied country variables and justify the selection of each proxy.

Following prior studies as for instance Watanabe et al. (2013) or Docherty and Hurst (2018), the first group of country characteristics serves as proxies for market efficiency and trading frictions. These characteristics are applied to test for causes which are exclusively related to deviating national market environments. That is, they are applied to analyze whether reported differences in (composite-enhanced) momentum returns are not related to theoretical models of investor over- or underreaction but rather due to market inefficiencies and frictions.

We apply four measures to account for market efficiency and limits to arbitrage: DEV, MCAP, EFR, and SHORT. DEV serves as an indicator for developed markets based on Morgan Stanley Capital International (MSCI) classifications and has been applied in prior cross-country studies as for instance Watanabe et al. (2013). Given that multiple studies (as for instance Bekaert and Harvey (2002)) argue that market inefficiencies might be higher in non-developed markets, a corresponding dummy variable is included within cross-country analyses below. MCAP indicates a country's stock market capitalization to GDP and is taken from the World Bank Financial Development Database. Following the rationale provided by La Porta et al. (1997), higher ratios of market capitalizaiton of publicly listed companies to GDP imply more developed and efficient financial markets. The Overall Economic Freedom Ranking Scores (EFR) as a measure of restrictions to capital flows is taken from the Fraser Institute. Corresponding scores are available online at https://www.fraserinstitute.org/. Similar variables have been applied in prior academic studies as for instance by Chan et al. (2005). The rationale beyond is that capital controls might narrow foreign capital flows of sophisticated investors, thus serving as a limit to arbitraging away mispricings. The last proxy for market efficiency and limits to arbitrage is taken from Bris et al. (2007). SHORT is a measure that equals 0 if short-selling is prohibited within a country, 1 if short-selling is allowed. Within their study, Bris et al. (2007) find markets to be more efficient whenever short-selling is allowed and practiced. As within our study we apply long-short strategy returns, accounting for short-sale permissions is of specific importance.

Second, we account for cross-country cultural differences. To do so, we use the six cultural dimensions by Hofstede et al. (2010): INDIV, MASC, PD, UA, LTO, and INDUL. Individualism (INDIV) stands for the extent to which people feel independent as opposed to being integrated into groups (Collectivism). Members of individualistic cultures are assumed to rather look after themselves than others (Hofstede, 2011). Also, and as for instance argued by Chui et al. (2010), INDIV is related to investor overconfidence and self-attribution bias. If composite-enhanced momentum returns are found to be higher in high-individualistic countries, we thus infer the results to be empirical evidence for overreaction-based momentum explanations as for instance the one provided by Daniel et al. (1998). Long-Term Orientation (LTO) illustrates the degree to which a society agrees that the world is in permanent change, implying that preparation for the future is essentially and always needed. LTO is associated with values such as thrift and perseverance (Hofstede, 2011). Prior works as for instance the study by Docherty and Hurst (2018) imply that there exists a negative link between LTO and momentum.[13] If composite-enhanced momentum returns are found to be smaller in high LTO countries, we thus interpret our findings as empirical evidence for the rationale that composite-enhanced momentum is driven by myopic investors focusing on short-term price fluctuations rather than firm fundamentals (as argued by Docherty and Hurst (2018) for ordinary momentum returns). The remaining cultural dimensions of Hofstede et al. (2010) are applied as control variables. Masculinity (MASC) reflects the distribution of values between genders. That is, to which either masculine (assertive) or feminine (modest and caring) gender-specific values are pervasive within a society. Power Distance (PD) refers to the degree to which the less powerful accept unequally distributed power. Uncertainty Avoidance (UA) indicates the extent of a society's tolerance for uncertainty and ambiguity. That is, to what degree a society tries to avoid unknown and surprising situations. Finally, the sixth cultural dimension which has been incorporated post hoc by Hofstede et al. (2010), is Indulgence (INDUL). INDUL refers to the extent to which a society accepts relatively free gratification as opposed to suppressing natural impulses through strict social norms (Hofstede, 2011).

Third, to test for quality and speed of information diffusion, we apply the following prox-

---

[13]Please note that Docherty and Hurst (2018) report a positive link between investor myopia and momentum. Among others, they apply the inverse of the LTO variable by Hofstede (2001) to construct the myopia index. We therefore hypothesize a negative link between LTO and momentum.

ies: Earnings Management Score (EMS) to measure information quality; the Opacity Index (OPA) developed by Kurtzman et al. (2004) as a proxy for information opaqueness as well as the number of news articles (NEWS). Corresponding EMS values are obtained from Leuz et al. (2003). The rationale beyond inclusion of this proxy is that we hypothesize a fast diffusion of information whenever information quality tends to be high. For instance, the study by You and Zhang (2009) finds the diffusion speed to be slower in markets exhibiting lower levels of information readability. The logic behind inclusion of the variable OPA is that information uncertainty is assumed to be higher within high opaque market environments. Higher information uncertainty in turn implies that stock prices are less likely to fully reflect all available information immediately, with markets thus exhibiting slower speed of information diffusion. We therefore argue that a potentially positive link between OPA and composite-enhanced momentum returns should be considered as empirical evidence for the slow diffusion model by Hong and Stein (1999). NEWS indicates the number of news articles scaled by the number of firms per country. Corresponding data is taken from Griffin et al. (2011). We consider the number of news articles to be a good proxy for information production, assuming that more available information should either result in more efficient markets or in less efficient markets (given potential disparity in information or potential information overload).

Lastly, to account for the role of fund flows for composite-enhanced momentum, we additionally incorporate the following two variables: MFA and PFA. Both variables are taken from the World Bank Financial Development Database. MFA stands for a country's Mutual Fund Assets to GDP. Mutual funds are considered to be any type of collective investment scheme pooling many from multiple investors to acquire securities. In a similar vein, PFA indicates the ratio of a nation's pension fund assets to GDP.[14] Both variables are included to approximate the model by Vayanos and Woolley (2013). Vayanos and Woolley (2013) argue that momentum arises if (active) fund flows exhibit inertia and prices underreact to expected future flows. We thus hypothesize as follows: The higher the amount of investment funds within a country, the greater the amount of funds gradually outflowing an asset whenever a negative shock impacts the fundamental value of this asset. Following the model by Vayanos

---

[14]Corresponding variable definitions are taken from the World Bank Financial Development Database itself.

and Woolley (2013), we further argue that this depresses the corresponding asset price, thus leading to momentum which is our comprehension and justification beyond inclusion of the proxies MFA and PFA.

Table 2.6 summarizes reported country variables for our chosen set of thirty-five countries. With the exception of EFR, MFA, PFA, and MCAP, applied proxies are time-invariant. For averages of time-series variables, the sample period is from January 1989 to December 2017 due to international data availability issues.

As illustrated, our sample contains 19 developed markets (DEV=1) for which the EFR variable tends to be higher accordingly. MCAP ranges from lowest 19.40% (Pakistan) to highest 562.14% (Hong Kong). Short-selling is prohibited within seven out of thirty-five countries.

Lowest EMS values are reported for China (1.00), the U.S. (2.00), and South Africa (5.60), highest EMS values are shown for Greece (28.30), South Korea (26.80) as well as Italy (24.80). Information opaqueness tends to be highest in Indonesia (59), China (50) and the Philippines (50), whereas it is lowest in Finland (13), Denmark (19), Sweden (19), and United Kingdom (19). The number of news articles (NEWS) is greatest in the U.S. (183,749), India (57,404), and Spain (53,052). Lowest NEWS values are shown for Canada (2,178), Brazil (3,341), and United Kingdom (3,695).

Similarly, MFA is highest in developed markets. Within our sample, highest average MFA figures are reported for Singapore (408.47), Hong Kong (383.03), and Australia (73.21). Lowest MFA values are observed within the Philippines (1.16), Pakistan (1.38), and Turkey (2.43). Highest average PFA figures are reported for Netherlands (125.51), Switzerland (103.86), and the U.S. market (95.59), whereas lowest values occur within Pakistan (0.03), Greece (0.31), and China (0.85).

Table 2.6: Applied Country Characteristics

This table reports country characteristics of our chosen set of 35 countries. Listed characteristics are used in the cross-country analyses of enhanced momentum returns. Our chosen set of country characteristics proxies for market efficiency, limits to arbitrage, cultural difference, speed and quality of information diffusion as well as the role of fund flows. Detailed variable definitions and data sources are provided in Appendix A.2 of the Electronic Supplementary Material. The table contains the following cross-sectional characteristics: DEV, SHORT, EMS, OPA, NEWS, INDIV, MASC, PD, UA, INDUL, and LTO. The following proxies illustrate averages of time-series variables: EFR, MFA, PFA, and MCAP. For averages of time-series variables, the sample period is from January 1989 to December 2017. Proxies for market efficiency and limits to arbitrage comprise DEV, MCAP, EFR, and SHORT. Proxies for cultural differences include INDIV, MASC, PD, UA, INDUL, and LTO. EMS, OPA, and NEWS are applied to account for quality and speed of information diffusion. Lastly, to account for the role of (active) fund flows, we incorporate MFA and PFA.

Country	DEV	EFR	MFA	PFA	MCAP	SHORT	EMS	OPA	NEWS	INDIV	MASC	PD	UA	INDUL	LTO
atl	1	8.00	73.21	90.73	87.91	1	4.80	21	6155	90	61	38	51	71	21
bel	0	7.51	30.81	4.98	57.79	1	19.50	23	13163	75	54	65	94	57	82
bra	0	5.86	40.22	13.29	33.76	1		40	3341	38	49	69	76	59	44
can	1	8.08	44.48	63.80	114.53	1	5.30	23	2178	80	52	39	48	68	36
chi	0	7.63	10.39	50.66	87.94	1		29	10554	23	28	63	86	68	31
chn	0	5.99	8.09	0.85	36.86	0	1.00	50	31255	20	66	80	30	24	87
den	1	7.82	29.08	36.80	48.94	1	16.00	19	13198	74	16	18	23	70	35
fin	1	7.80	26.21	62.39	78.39	1	12.00	13	14064	63	26	33	59	57	38
fra	1	7.32	61.48	6.72	63.15	1	13.50	37	4685	71	43	68	86	48	63
ger	1	7.77	43.22	5.12	38.91	1	21.50	25	15878	67	66	35	65	40	83
gre	0	6.85	6.38	0.31	35.04	0	28.30	41	5496	35	57	60	112	50	45
hkg	0	8.91	383.03	29.74	562.14	1	19.50	20	22944	25	57	68	29	17	61
ido	0	6.53	4.50	1.89	27.04	0	18.30	59	4949	14	46	78	48	38	62
ind	0	6.38	6.35	1.57	48.34	0	19.10	48	57404	48	56	77	40	26	51
ita	1	7.25	18.22	4.97	30.54	1	24.80	43	34864	76	70	50	75	30	61
jap	1	7.77	27.86	26.45	77.66	1	20.50	42	7932	46	95	54	92	42	88
mal	0	6.90	22.98	51.64	144.96	1	14.80	35	21202	26	50	104	36	57	41
mex	0	6.57	6.89	8.86	26.84	1		44	8067	30	69	81	82	97	24
net	1	7.78	58.16	125.51	84.27	1	16.50	24	21702	80	14	38	53	68	67
nor	1	7.52	18.93	7.39	41.77	1	5.80		12163	69	8	31	50	55	35
nzl	1	8.32	15.27	17.14	36.64	1			13119	79	58	22	49	75	33
pak	0	5.77	1.38	0.03	19.40	0	17.80	45	7646	14	50	55	70	0	50
phi	0	6.93	1.16	3.53	52.75	1	8.80	50	6246	32	64	94	44	42	27
pol	0	6.67	3.72	9.67	21.12	1		41	17963	60	64	68	93	29	38
sin	1	8.57	408.47	36.56	175.01	0	21.60	24	23669	20	48	74	8	46	72
soa	0	6.65	30.91	89.07	184.75	1	5.60	34	11898	65	63	49	49	63	34
sok	0	7.27	8.60		77.69	0	26.80	37		18	39	60	85	29	100
spa	1	7.49	23.47	7.74	60.70	1	18.60	34	53052	51	42	57	86	44	48
swe	1	7.61	50.64	45.73	82.39	1	6.80	19	16667	71	5	31	29	78	53
swi	1	8.42	42.76	103.86	177.38	1	22.00	23	13225	68	70	34	58	66	74
tai	0	7.49				0	22.50	34	46700	17	45	58	69	49	93
tha	0	6.69	15.98	5.30	60.27	1	18.30	35	11760	20	34	64	64	45	32
tur	0	6.37	2.43	1.07	19.96	1		43	10822	37	45	66	85	49	46
uni	1	8.14	28.53	79.71	111.95	1	7.00	19	3695	89	66	35	35	69	51
usa	1	8.21	68.32	95.59	110.82	1	2.00	21	183749	91	62	40	46	68	26

2.5.2   Cross-Sectional Regressions

We strive to analyze causes of global differences in composite-enhanced momentum returns. Beyond, we aim to study whether drivers of composite-enhanced momentum returns deviate from drivers of ordinary momentum returns. In the regression analyses below, our dependent variable thus either constitutes the country-level ordinary momentum return or the country-level composite-enhanced momentum return. These momentum variables have two dimensions: country and time, thus exhibiting a panel data structure. Reported country characteristics as outlined in Section 2.5.1, in part exhibit a panel data structure. In part, however, they only exhibit the country-dimension, i.e. they are time-invariant. To account for this disparity in data structure, we apply averages of time-series country variables and exclusively apply cross-sectional regressions below. Due to international data availability issues of specific country variables, the sample period for cross-sectional regressions is limited from January 1989 to December 2017.

In doing so, we measure the between-effect (see e.g. Watanabe et al. (2013)). That is, we study drivers of differences in cross-country (composite-enhanced) momentum returns. Accordingly, the dependent variable is either the time-series average of country-specific ordinary momentum or the time-series average of country-specific composite-enhanced momentum return as outlined in Section 2.4.3. As independent variables we apply both, time-invariant and time-series averages of corresponding country characteristics described in Section 2.5.1.

Tables 2.7 to 2.9 summarize empirical findings for multiple cross-sectional regression specifications. Within each table, Panel A reports findings for cross-country differences in ordinary momentum returns. Panel B shows explanations with regard to cross-country differences in composite-enhanced momentum returns.

Table 2.7: Cross-Country Analyses:
Market Efficiency and Trading Frictions

This table summarizes empirical findings of cross-sectional regressions studying drivers of global differences for ordinary and composite-enhanced momentum returns. As dependent variable, we apply country-specific time-series averages of ordinary momentum returns (Panel A) as well as time-series averages of composite-enhanced momentum returns (Panel B). As independent variables, we apply our proxies for market efficiency and trading frictions. DEV is an indicator variable for developed markets. MCAP indicates the time-series average of a country's stock market capitalization to GDP. EFR stands for the time-series average of a country's economic freedom ranking score. SHORT is an indicator variable with regard to the allowance of short-selling. For illustration purposes, all coefficients are multiplied by 100. t-statistics are indicated within parentheses. The sample period runs from M1:1989 to M12:2017 due to availability of international country variables data. *, **, and *** indicate statistical significance at the 10%, 5%, and 1% level.

	Model 1	Model 2	Model 3	Model 4	Model 5
Panel A: Ordinary Momentum					
DEV	0.1360				-0.1356
	(1.05)				(-0.56)
MCAP		-0.0001			-0.0006
		(-0.14)			(-0.69)
EFR			0.0866		0.1390
			(1.01)		(0.80)
SHORT				0.3099**	0.3140*
				(2.01)	(1.77)
Intercept	0.5648***	0.6573***	-0.0054	0.3907***	-0.5068
	(5.93)	(7.21)	(-0.01)	(2.83)	(-0.44)
R^2	0.0325	0.0006	0.0298	0.1088	0.1435
Panel B: Composite-Enhanced Momentum					
DEV	0.3215**				0.4399
	(2.04)				(1.42)
MCAP		-0.0004			-0.0007
		(-0.44)			(-0.67)
EFR			0.1298		-0.0693
			(1.19)		(-0.31)
SHORT				0.2337	0.0592
				(1.14)	(0.26)
Intercept	0.4337***	0.6407 ***	-0.3565	0.4212**	0.8915
	(3.73)	(5.47)	(-0.44)	(2.31)	(0.61)
R^2	0.112	0.006	0.0412	0.0382	0.1546

Table 2.8: Cross-Country Analyses: Cultural Dimensions

This table summarizes empirical findings of cross-sectional regressions studying drivers of global differences for ordinary and composite-enhanced momentum returns. As dependent variable, we apply country-specific time-series averages of ordinary momentum returns (Panel A) as well as time-series averages of composite-enhanced momentum returns (Panel B). As independent variables, we apply our proxies for cross-country cultural differences. These proxies comprise the six cultural dimensions by Hofstede: individualism (INDIV), masculinity (MASC), power distance (PD), uncertainty avoidance (UA), indulgence (INDUL), long-term orientation (LTO). For illustration purposes, all coefficients are multiplied by 100. t-statistics are indicated within parentheses. The sample period runs from M1:1989 to M12:2017 due to comparability reasons regarding remaining cross-sectional country regressions. *, **, and *** indicate statistical significance at the 10%, 5%, and 1% level.

	Model 1	Model 2	Model 3	Model 4	Model 5	Model 6	Model 7
Panel A: Ordinary Momentum							
INDIV	0.0069***						0.0050
	(2.99)						(1.34)
MASC		-0.0034					-0.0022
		(-1.00)					(-0.63)
PD			-0.0066**				-0.0014
			(-2.15)				(-0.31)
UA				0.0008			0.0023
				(0.28)			(0.90)
INDUL					0.0068**		0.0003
					(2.15)		(0.09)
LTO						-0.0072**	-0.0055*
						(-2.59)	(-1.76)
Intercept	0.2884**	0.8045***	1.0076***	0.5887***	0.2922*	1.0175***	0.7085
	(2.21)	(4.43)	(5.47)	(3.26)	(1.70)	(6.44)	(1.41)
R^2	0.2130	0.0304	0.1262	0.0024	0.1230	0.1689	0.3402
Panel B: Composite-Enhanced Momentum							
INDIV	0.0065**						-0.0001
	(2.09)						(-0.03)
MASC		-0.0007					0.0018
		(-0.15)					(0.43)
PD			-0.0104***				-0.0080
			(-2.75)				(-1.47)
UA				0.0026			0.0031
				(0.74)			(1.03)
INDUL					0.0097**		0.0116**
					(2.46)		(2.59)
LTO						0.0044	0.0085**
						(1.15)	(2.28)
Intercept	0.2783	0.6467***	1.1968***	0.4591**	0.1129	0.3779*	-0.2473
	(1.58)	(2.76)	(5.31)	(2.01)	(0.52)	(1.75)	(-0.41)
R^2	0.1166	0.0007	0.1907	0.0166	0.1551	0.0385	0.4231

Table 2.9: Cross-Country Analyses:
Information Quality and Diffusion Speed

This table summarizes empirical findings of cross-sectional regressions studying drivers of global differences for ordinary and composite-enhanced momentum returns. As dependent variable, we apply country-specific time-series averages of ordinary momentum returns (Panel A) as well as time-series averages of composite-enhanced momentum returns (Panel B). As independent variables, we apply our proxies for information quality and diffusion speed. The earnings management score (EMS) is a proxy for information quality. The opacity index (OPA) indicates the degree of information opaqueness. NEWS stands for the number of news articles scaled by the number of firms per country. For illustration purposes, all coefficients are multiplied by 100. t-statistics are indicated within parentheses. The sample period runs from M1:1989 to M12:2017 due to comparability reasons regarding remaining cross-sectional country regressions. *, **, and *** indicate statistical significance at the 10%, 5%, and 1% level.

	Model 1	Model 2	Model 3	Model 4
Panel A: Ordinary Momentum				
EMS	-0.00126			0.00412
	(-0.14)			(0.45)
OPA		-0.0097*		-0.0131**
		(-1.70)		(-2.36)
NEWS			-0.0000	-0.0000
			(-1.28)	(-1.20)
Intercept	0.6160***	0.9338***	0.7038***	0.9922***
	(4.08)	(4.71)	(8.88)	(4.37)
R^2	0.0007	0.085	0.049	0.2309
Panel B: Composite-Enhanced Momentum				
EMS	0.0044			0.0122
	(0.38)			(0.98)
OPA		-0.0137*		-0.0147*
		(-1.87)		(-1.94)
NEWS			0.0000	0.0000
			(0.35)	(0.55)
Intercept	0.5658***	1.0345***	0.5837***	0.8564***
	(2.91)	(4.08)	(5.62)	(2.76)
R^2	0.0054	0.1016	0.0039	0.1641

Table 2.7 starts by summarizing findings when applying proxies for market efficiency and trading frictions. The results in Panel A show that ordinary momentum returns tend to be higher within countries that allow and practice short-selling (statistical significance at the 5%-level within univariate regression). When controlling for other proxies of market efficiency and trading frictions, the variable SHORT remains statistically significant (at the 10%-level) in explaining ordinary momentum returns. Additionally, the results imply that the proxies DEV, MCAP, and EFR have no explanatory power for ordinary momentum returns. Conversely, with regard to cross-country differences in composite-enhanced momentum returns (Panel B), DEV is the only proxy exhibiting (positive) explanatory power (at the 5%-level). In the multivariate regressions (where DEV, MCAP, EFR, and SHORT are applied jointly), however, the explanatory power of DEV for composite-enhanced momentum returns disappears.

We continue by analyzing the relation between (composite-enhanced) momentum and the six cultural dimensions by Hofstede et al. (2010). Table 2.8 summarizes corresponding results. The univariate regression results indicate that there exists a positive relationship between ordinary momentum returns and individualism (t-statics of 2.99). This finding is in line with prior research (Chui et al., 2010). Beyond, we find a positive link between ordinary momentum and indulgence (t-statistics of 2.15) and negative relations between ordinary momentum and power distance (t-statistic of -2.15) as well as negative relations between ordinary momentum and long-term orientation (t-statistics of -2.59). When applying multivariate regression analysis comprising the six dimensions simultaneously, the explanatory power of the proxies INDIV, INDUL, and PD for ordinary momentum disappears entirely. We attribute this pattern to potential multicollinearity issues.[15] Still, LTO remains significant even within multivariate regression analysis (t-statistic of -1.76). When applying average composite-enhanced momentum returns as dependent variable in univariate regressions (Panel B), we find that individualism (t-statistics of 2.09) and indulgence (t-statistics of 2.46) exhibit positive significance in explaining cross-country differences. Also, PD has negative significance in explaining composite-enhanced momentum returns within the uni-

---

[15]For instance, as shown in Appendix A.3 of the Electronic Supplementary Material, the correlation coefficient between INDIV and PD equals -0.72. Once excluding PD from the multivariate regression, INDIV again becomes statistically significant at the 5%-level.

variate regressions (t-statistics of -2.75). Beyond, multivariate regression results reveal that out of these proxies, indulgence is the only one to maintain its statistical significance. Opposed to this, INDIV and PD become insignificant in the multivariate regression. Again, this finding is to be considered with caution due to multicollinearity issues between the six cultural dimensions.

With regard to our proxies for information quality and diffusion speed, reported results in Table 2.9 imply a negative link between both, ordinary and composite-enhanced momentum returns and the opacity index. The EMS and NEWS variables are insignificant within the univariate regressions. When applying the three proxies jointly, we find the overall results to be unaffected. That is, multivariate regressions in both panels indicate a negative link between the dependent variable and the opacity index, whereas EMS and NEWS again have no explanatory power.

When applying univariate regressions for our proxies of fund flows (MFA, PFA), we obtain insignificant results for both, ordinary and composite-enhanced momentum returns. We therefore refrain from summarizing corresponding figures within this paper.

2.5.3 Competing Explanations of (Composite-Enhanced) Momentum

As of now, we exclusively have applied univariate regressions to test for the impact of each country characteristic upon both, ordinary and composite-enhanced momentum. Beyond, we have applied multivariate regressions for each group of country characteristics accordingly. As emphasized by Watanabe et al. (2013), a reasonable concern arising thereof is that potential correlations among applied (groups of) country characteristics might impact findings reported in Section 2.5.2.[16] Therefore, to test for the robustness of reported findings as well as to evaluate the relative importance of previously found significant proxies and thus potential momentum explanations, we proceed by applying multivariate regression analyses below.

Again, as dependent variables we apply the country-specific time-series average of ordinary

---

[16]Correlations of applied country characteristics are shown in Appendix A.3 of the Electronic Supplementary Material.

momentum returns or the country-specific time-series average of composite-enhanced momentum returns. As independent variables, we apply the proxies SHORT, INDIV, and OPA with regard to ordinary momentum. For composite-enhanced momentum, we account for DEV, INDIV, PD, and OPA. These proxies are chosen as they have shown highest statistical significance within univariate regressions. In the following analyses, following the approach by Watanabe et al. (2013), they are then paired with all other country characteristics, one at a time. As emphasized above, these steps are necessary to test for robustness and relative explanatory importance. In doing so, we simultaneously study which momentum model best fits our empirical findings.

Table 2.10 shows corresponding findings for ordinary momentum returns. Table 2.11 summarizes findings obtained for composite-enhanced momentum returns.

Most importantly, the results reported in Table 2.10 corroborate the robustness of the individualism proxy for ordinary momentum returns. Within each regression specification, INDIV remains relevant, at least at the 10% level. Conversely, the SHORT variable remains only significant within seven out of twelve regression specifications. Once applying INDIV and SHORT jointly, SHORT becomes insignificant whereas INDIV is relevant at the 5% level despite potential multicollinearity issues (correlation coefficient of 0.70). In a similar vein, the OPA variable remains relevant in explaining ordinary momentum returns within seven out of twelve regression specifications. Once applying OPA and INDIV jointly, OPA becomes insignificant whereas INDIV remains relevant at the 1%-level. Therefore, these findings emphasize that ordinary momentum returns tend to be higher in markets that practice short-selling, while simultaneously exhibiting less information opaqueness and above all higher degrees of investor overconfidence.

For composite-enhanced momentum returns, Table 2.11 shows that both, DEV, INDIV, and PD jointly are most significant in explaining global differences. The OPA variable remains negatively relevant in explaining composite-enhanced momentum returns within seven out of twelve regression specificiations.

Table 2.10: Cross-Country Analyses of Ordinary Momentum:
Robustness Tests

This table shows results of cross-country regressions examining the effect of the previously found significant variables SHORT (Panel A), INDIV (Panel B), and OPA (Panel C) jointly with other measures of market efficiency, cultural differences as well as further measures of quality and speed of information diffusion. The dependent variable is the within-country time-series average of ordinary momentum returns. For illustration purposes, all coefficients are multiplied by 100. t-statistics are indicated within parentheses. *, **, and *** indicate statistical significance at the 10%, 5% as well as 1% level.

| | Panel A: SHORT Against Alternatives | | | | | | | | | | | |
	Model 1	Model 2	Model 3	Model 4	Model 5	Model 6	Model 7	Model 8	Model 9	Model 10	Model 11	Model 12
SHORT	0.28842*	0.3281**	0.2885*	0.08123	0.30149*	0.20266	0.30634*	0.20814	0.21235	0.28298*	0.21166	0.33007**
	(1.69)	(2.09)	(1.73)	(0.45)	(1.91)	(1.19)	(1.91)	(1.24)	(1.38)	(1.82)	(1.24)	(2.01)
DEV	0.04298											
	(0.31)											
MCAP		0.00020										
		(-0.29)										
EFR			0.03258									
			(0.37)									
INDIV				0.00612**								
				(2.11)								
MASC					-0.00317							
					(-0.96)							
PD						-0.00494						
						(-1.46)						
UA							0.00024					
							(0.09)					
INDUL								0.00496				
								(1.45)				
LTO									-0.00603**			
									(-2.08)			
EMS										0.00261		
										(0.30)		
OPA											-0.00659	
											(-1.06)	
NEWS												0.00000
												(-1.51)
INTERCEPT	0.35455***	0.4054***	0.16564	0.2623*	0.55204**	0.7513*	0.37717*	0.21768	0.78442***	0.34271	0.66451**	0.43942***
	(2.72)	(2.73)	(0.26)	(1.81)	(2.52)	(2.65)	(1.83)	(1.20)	(3.41)	(1.64)	(2.27)	(2.89)
R^2	0.1115	0.124	0.1125	0.2179	0.1327	0.1642	0.1071	0.1634	0.2153	0.1132	0.1294	0.1586

Table 2.10 (Cont'd)

| | | | | | Panel B: INDIV Against Alternatives | | | | | | | |
	Model 1	Model 2	Model 3	Model 4	Model 5	Model 6	Model 7	Model 8	Model 9	Model 10	Model 11	Model 12
INDIV	0.01033***	0.00671***	0.00741***	0.00612**	0.00679***	0.0062*	0.00699***	0.00568**	0.00573**	0.00863***	0.00583*	0.00773***
	(3.16)	(2.75)	(2.77)	(2.11)	(2.89)	(1.85)	(2.93)	(2.15)	(2.54)	(3.67)	(1.95)	(3.32)
DEV	-0.24181											
	(-1.46)											
MCAP		0.00005										
		(0.08)										
EFR			-0.03599									
			(-0.40)									
SHORT				0.08123								
				(0.45)								
MASC					-0.00313							
					(-1.01)							
PD						-0.00119						
						(-0.28)						
UA							0.00144					
							(0.58)					
INDCL								0.00318				
								(0.93)				
LTO									-0.00559**			
									(-2.09)			
EMS										0.01117		
										(1.38)		
OPA											-0.00214	
											(-0.32)	
NEWS												0.00383**
												(-2.06)
INTERCEPT	0.24396*	0.29573*	0.52918	0.2623*	0.44693**	0.38895	0.19485	0.18654	0.63962***	-0.02295	0.39699	0.32758**
	(1.85)	(1.90)	(0.86)	(1.81)	(2.18)	(1.03)	(0.93)	(1.09)	(3.06)	(-0.11)	(1.19)	(2.47)
R^2	0.2622	0.1961	0.2169	0.2179	0.2361	0.2129	0.2192	0.2338	0.3079	0.342	0.1879	0.2988

Table 2.10 (Cont'd)

Panel C: OPA Against Alternatives

	Model 1	Model 2	Model 3	Model 4	Model 5	Model 6	Model 7	Model 8	Model 9	Model 10	Model 11	Model 12
OPA	-0.01511*	-0.01168*	-0.01853*	-0.00659	-0.00214	-0.00922	-0.00577	-0.01125*	-0.00602	-0.00947*	-0.01292**	-0.01041*
	(-1.71)	(-1.82)	(-1.86)	(-1.06)	(-0.32)	(-1.51)	(-0.70)	(-1.87)	(-0.94)	(-1.77)	(-2.35)	(-1.81)
DEV	-0.15987											
	(-0.80)											
MCAP		-0.00057										
		(-0.74)										
EFR			-0.16143									
			(-1.08)									
SHORT				0.21166								
				(1.24)								
INDIV					0.00583*							
					(1.95)							
MASC						-0.00131						
						(-0.35)						
PD							-0.00333					
							(-0.70)					
UA								0.0026				
								(0.94)				
INDUL									0.00463			
									(1.27)			
LTO										-0.0065**		
										(-2.32)		
EMS											0.00489	
											(0.57)	
NEWS												0.00000
												(-1.42)
INTERCEPT	1.19286***	1.05917***	2.41689*	0.66451**	0.39699	0.97873***	0.99301***	0.8205***	0.57887*	1.27326***	0.91384***	1.02624***
	(3.14)	(4.12)	(1.74)	(2.27)	(1.19)	(3.96)	(4.47)	(3.52)	(1.69)	(5.38)	(4.39)	(4.93)
R^2	0.1042	0.1023	0.1193	0.1294	0.1879	0.0899	0.1011	0.113	0.1316	0.2239	0.1814	0.1417

Table 2.11: Cross-Country Analyses of Composite-Enhanced Momentum: Robustness Tests

This table shows results of cross-country regressions examining the effect of the previously found significant variables DEV (Panel A), INDIV (Panel B), PD (Panel C) and OPA (Panel D) jointly with other measures of market efficiency, cultural differences as well as further measures of quality and speed of information diffusion. The dependent variable is the within-country time-series average of composite-enhanced momentum returns. For illustration purposes, all coefficients are multiplied by 100. t-statistics are indicated within parentheses. *, **, and *** indicate statistical significance at the 10%, 5% as well as 1% level.

| | Panel A: DEV Against Alternatives | | | | | | | | | | | |
	Model 1	Model 2	Model 3	Model 4	Model 5	Model 6	Model 7	Model 8	Model 9	Model 10	Model 11	Model 12
DEV	0.38373**	0.44887*	0.29341*	0.17675	0.31833*	0.05036	0.35222**	0.23396	0.30735*	0.31688*	0.14327	0.33927**
	(2.29)	(1.72)	(1.68)	(0.77)	(1.92)	(0.23)	(2.29)	(1.49)	(1.94)	(1.83)	(0.56)	(2.05)
MCAP	-0.00093											
	(-1.04)											
EFR		-0.10688										
		(-0.62)										
SHORT			0.08704									
			(0.40)									
INDIV				0.00396								
				(0.88)								
MASC					-0.00007							
					(-0.02)							
PD						-0.00954*						
						(-1.81)						
UA							0.00473					
							(1.38)					
INDUL								0.00799**				
								(1.99)				
LTO									0.00377			
									(1.02)			
EMS										0.00723		
										(0.65)		
OPA											-0.00887	
											(-0.78)	
NEWS												0.00000
												(0.11)
INTERCEPT	0.47215***	1.15913	0.37926*	0.31073*	0.44028*	1.12142***	0.11516	0.07156	0.24377	0.32623	0.80224*	0.40891***
	(3.56)	(0.98)	(2.11)	(1.70)	(1.76)	(2.83)	(0.44)	(0.34)	(1.11)	(1.43)	(1.65)	(3.13)
R^2	0.1499	0.1224	0.1164	0.1327	0.1067	0.1922	0.1586	0.2097	0.1401	0.1186	0.1109	0.1225

Table 2.11 (Cont'd)

	Model 1	Model 2	Model 3	Model 4	Model 5	Model 6	Model 7	Model 8	Model 9	Model 10	Model 11	Model 12
						Panel B: INDIV Against Alternatives						
INDIV	0.00396	0.00691**	0.00605*	0.0066*	0.00667**	0.00167	0.00697**	0.00372	0.00785**	0.00974***	0.00373	0.00704**
	(0.88)	(2.11)	(1.67)	(1.69)	(2.09)	(0.39)	(2.20)	(1.07)	(2.54)	(3.04)	(0.93)	(2.12)
DEV	0.17675											
	(0.77)											
MCAP		-0.00025										
		(-0.28)										
EFR			0.02963									
			(0.24)									
SHORT				-0.01319								
				(-0.05)								
MASC					-0.00035							
					(-0.08)							
PD						-0.00591*						
						(-1.65)						
UA							0.00324					
							(0.98)					
INDUL								0.00732				
								(1.63)				
LTO									0.00665*			
									(1.82)			
EMS										0.01843*		
										(1.66)		
OPA											-0.00886	
											(-0.99)	
NEWS												0.00000
												(-0.03)
INTERCEPT	0.31073*	0.26853	0.07997	0.2825	0.29495	1.03013**	0.06669	0.04371	-0.13971	-0.15551	0.69092	0.24084
	(1.70)	(1.29)	(0.10)	(1.44)	(1.06)	(2.11)	(0.24)	(0.19)	(-0.49)	(-0.53)	(1.54)	(1.27)
R^2	0.1327	0.1308	0.1182	0.1166	0.1238	0.1946	0.1498	0.1843	0.1994	0.2663	0.127	0.1304

Table 2.11 (Cont'd)

						Panel C: PD Against Alternatives						
	Model 1	Model 2	Model 3	Model 4	Model 5	Model 6	Model 7	Model 8	Model 9	Model 10	Model 11	Model 12
PD	-0.00954*	-0.01034**	-0.01129**	-0.01015**	-0.00891*	-0.01113***	-0.01088***	-0.00791**	-0.01076***	-0.01115***	-0.00897	-0.01038***
	(-1.81)	(-2.65)	(-2.45)	(-2.40)	(-1.65)	(-2.79)	(-2.87)	(-2.00)	(-2.88)	(-2.84)	(-1.51)	(-2.66)
DEV	0.05036											
	(0.23)											
MCAP		-0.00020										
		(-0.23)										
EFR			-0.04473									
			(-0.36)									
SHORT				0.02742								
				(0.13)								
INDIV					0.00167							
					(0.39)							
MASC						0.00275						
						(0.65)						
UA							0.00364					
							(1.14)					
INDUL								0.00696*				
								(1.70)				
LTO									0.00498			
									(1.40)			
EMS										0.00836		
										(0.77)		
OPA											-0.0029	
											(-0.29)	
NEWS												0.00000
												(0.20)
INTERCEPT	1.12142***	1.20818***	1.58141	1.16207***	1.03013**	1.10364***	1.00522***	0.70384*	0.95481***	1.12397***	1.20643***	1.18098***
	(2.83)	(5.03)	(1.44)	(3.28)	(2.11)	(4.11)	(3.59)	(1.94)	(3.39)	(4.29)	(4.38)	(4.88)
R^2	0.1922	0.1928	0.1941	0.1912	0.1946	0.2018	0.2235	0.26	0.2391	0.2457	0.1666	0.1936

Table 2.11 (Cont'd)

						Panel D: OPA Against Alternatives						
	Model 1	Model 2	Model 3	Model 4	Model 5	Model 6	Model 7	Model 8	Model 9	Model 10	Model 11	Model 12
OPA	-0.00887	-0.01811**	-0.02246*	-0.01272	-0.00886	-0.01492*	-0.0029	-0.01654**	-0.00786	-0.01392*	-0.01485**	-0.01372*
	(-0.78)	(-2.22)	(-1.75)	(-1.57)	(-0.99)	(-1.92)	(-0.29)	(-2.19)	(-0.98)	(-1.94)	(-2.03)	(-1.81)
DEV	0.14327											
	(0.56)											
MCAP		-0.00121										
		(-1.24)										
EFR			-0.16045									
			(-0.83)									
SHORT				0.06628								
				(0.30)								
INDIV					0.00373							
					(0.93)							
MASC						0.00309						
						(0.64)						
PD							-0.00897					
							(-1.51)					
UA								0.00504				
								(1.45)				
INDUL									0.00732			
									(1.59)			
LTO										0.00570		
										(1.52)		
EMS											0.01136	
											(1.00)	
NEWS												0.00000
												(0.24)
INTERCEPT	0.80224*	1.28444***	2.50864	0.95013**	0.69092	0.92425***	1.20643***	0.82477***	0.47426	0.73706**	0.91042***	1.01417***
	(1.65)	(3.94)	(1.41)	(2.48)	(1.54)	(2.94)	(4.38)	(2.82)	(1.10)	(2.33)	(3.29)	(3.69)
R^2	0.1109	0.1477	0.122	0.1043	0.127	0.114	0.1666	0.1622	0.1714	0.1657	0.1542	0.1065

The fact that we observe a negative link between OPA and both, ordinary as well as composite-enhanced momentum returns, seems contradictory to the slow diffusion model by Hong and Stein (1999). In fact, our results indicate that markets which exhibit greater opaqueness exhibit less momentum returns. Simultaneously, this implies that ordinary and composite-enhanced momentum returns are higher whenever we observe markets with clear, accurate, and easily discernible information (as described by Kurtzman et al. (2004)).

When it comes to our proxies for market efficiency, we find within multivariate regressions that for ordinary momentum returns, the explanatory power of INDIV is stronger than the explanatory power of SHORT as well as all other proxies for market efficiency or trading frictions. For composite-enhanced momentum returns, we find that both, market efficiency and cultural variables matter strongly. Specifically, the DEV and PD proxies are highly relevant in explaining returns obtained from our composite-enhanced momentum strategy. Whereas INDIV also matters for composite-momentum, we find the t-statistics of PD to be stronger in most regression specifications. This finding implies that composite-enhanced momentum returns are highest within developed, highly individualistic markets whose citizens are unwilling to accept unequally distributed power.

A reasonable question arising thereof is how power distance itself relates to behavioral biases such as investor overconfidence and how this link in turn relates to theoretical models of momentum. As of now, we are not aware of studies explicitly focusing on the link between power distance and momentum returns. However, we would like to emphasize that reported findings are broadly related to a study by Ferris et al. (2013), indicating that power distance is inversely related to CEO overconfidence. Yet, we acknowledge that the link between CEO overconfidence and power distance deviates from a (potential) link between investor overconfidence and power distance which is still subject to be confirmed empirically.

Beyond, the results for both, ordinary and composite-enhanced momentum returns are consistent with the fact that markets with higher levels of investor overconfidence (INDIV) tend to be markets with lower levels of information opaqueness (OPA). Specifically, the correlation between INDIV and OPA amounts to -0.61 within our sample.

Overall, we thus cautiously interpret our findings as supportive evidence for overreaction-based explanations as for instance the one by Daniel et al. (1998) for both, ordinary and composite-enhanced momentum.

2.6 Conclusion

Empirical evidence is far from conclusive on what drives both, ordinary and characteristics-enhanced momentum returns. This study takes a composite look on how firm-specific characteristics relate to momentum profits across the globe. Specifically, we constructe a composite-momentum metric that combines information from a variety of stock characteristics. These characteristics have individually been shown to enhance momentum returns in prior work.

We demonstrate that momentum profits are predictable across many international markets when combining information given in multiple stock characteristics. Predicted momentum profits are comparatively simple to compute, can yield significant positive out-of-sample portfolio returns, and cannot be explained by idiosyncratic volatility, extreme past returns or Carhart's four factors to its full extent.

Cross-country analyses reveal that both, ordinary and composite-enhanced momentum returns tend to be positively correlated, higher within countries that exhibit less trading frictions (i.e. developed markets with no short-sale constraints) and markets that exhibit less information opaqueness. Simultaneously, we find composite-enhanced momentum returns to be higher in highly individualistic countries that simultaneously exhibit smaller degrees of power distance. We cautiously interpret our findings as empirical support for overreaction-based explanations of ordinary and composite-enhanced momentum.

Chapter 3

Capital Share Risk in International Asset Pricing

This chapter introduces the second dissertation study which analyzes whether capital share growth is a priced risk factor across international equity markets.

Zusatzmaterial online
Zusätzliche Informationen sind in der Online-Version dieses Kapitel (https://doi.org/10.1007/978-3-658-35479-4_3) enthalten.

3.1   Introduction

In a seminal study, Lettau et al. (2019) demonstrate that a single macroeconomic factor can explain a wide range of equity and nonequity portfolio returns within the U.S. market. This factor, which is based on the growth in the capital share of aggregate income, is able to outperform, yet even subsume information in well-established factor models as for instance the Fama-French three factor model. The aim of this paper is to study whether the explanatory power of this factor maintains across international equity markets.

It is well acknowledged that international markets are important (Jacobs and Müller, 2020; Karolyi, 2016). By the end of 2017, U.S. firms accounted for approximately 35% of worldwide market capitalization, implying that 65% of the entire global equity market worth is attributable to international markets.[1] Beyond their importance in terms of absolute economic figures, international markets are explicitly relevant from a financial research perspective for at least two reasons.

First, they offer scientists the possibility to conduct broad international replications and out-of-sample tests. In doing so, they are an important tool for evaluating the relative importance and robustness of newly discovered asset pricing factors and anomalies. This seems particularly necessary given that throughout the past decades, a vast amount of new asset pricing factors and anomalies has inundated top finance journals. A trend that is increasingly associated with negative terms such as *p-hacking* (Harvey, 2017), *data mining* (Harvey et al., 2016), and *zoo of new factors* (Cochrane, 2011). In the anomaly literature, Hou et al. (2020a) for instance illustrate that the economic magnitude of the majority of 452 replicated anomalies is significantly smaller than reported in the corresponding reference studies. A result strikingly emphasizing the need for broad replication studies and broad out-of-sample tests.

Second, analyses of international markets enhance our understanding of what segments or integrates international equity markets (Bekaert et al., 2011; Bekaert and Harvey, 2017). Thus, they are inevitable for obtaining a holistic understanding of global capital markets

---

[1] Calculations are based upon our data set described in Section 3.3.

and asset price formation processes. Detecting differences in factor and anomaly estimates for international markets compared to those obtained for the U.S. market is the first crucial step in identifying drivers of global equity market segmentations. Indeed, a wide range of asset pricing studies finds that many patterns obtained within the U.S. deviate across international markets (Fama and French, 2012, 2017; Jacobs and Müller, 2018, 2020).

Given these recent developments, the primary aim of our study thus is to employ an extensive global data set to analyze the relative importance and robustness of the newly discovered capital share growth factor. In particular, we strive to answer the following research questions:

1. Is capital share growth a persistent and consistent driver of equity portfolio returns across global equity markets?

2. Are there differences and commonalities across countries and regions worldwide? What explains potential cross-country differences?

3. Is it possible to exploit the information contained in the capital share growth factor by a tradable (out-of-sample) investment strategy?

To answer these questions, we implement an analysis of 45 developed and emerging equity markets across the globe. Specifically, to ensure comprehensive and thorough, yet simultaneously solid and robust analyses, we restrict our sample to countries listed in the following regional indices: MSCI North America, MSCI Europe, MSCI Pacific, and MSCI Emerging Markets.

Our paper reports the following key results. First, we are able to replicate the results reported by Lettau et al. (2019) for the U.S. market in both, size and significance, thus dispersing potential p-hacking and data mining concerns. Second, we illustrate that capital share growth is a priced risk factor across international markets. There exists, however, strong geographic heterogeneity in the explanatory power of this factor. Pooled estimates reveal that capital share growth is particularly significant for Emerging Markets, while being less relevant for G7 + Australia (excl. USA). Unlike the U.S. market, though, the information contained in the KS risk factor of international markets does not subsume information contained in alternative factor models as for instance the Fama-French three factor or q-factor models, but rather adds additional explanatory content to these model specifications. Pooled estimates for G7 + Australia (excl. USA), however, reveal that the capital share factor is in part even entirely subsumed by alternative factor model specifications.

Third, capital share growth is a local rather than global risk factor. Once applying global capital share estimates, the explanatory power of the factor is substantially reduced and oftentimes disappears entirely. These results are in line with studies for instance conducted by Hollstein (2020) or Hou et al. (2011), implying that local factors exhibit greater explanatory power for international equity markets compared to global factor constructions.

Fourth, cross-sectional regression analysis reveals that cross-country differences in the explanatory power of local KS risk estimates can best be explained by variations in private wealth inequality as well as further macroeconomic variables as for instance variations in public wealth. These findings underpin the theoretical explanations given by Lettau et al. (2019) in an international setting: The smaller the amount of capital market risk beard by a given subset of investors, the smaller the expected compensation in terms of equity portfolio returns.

Lastly, we are able to illustrate that - while exhibiting great in-sample explanatory power and significance - the information contained in the capital share growth factor cannot be exploited out-of-sample. An investment strategy that goes long the decile of past capital share growth beta winners and short the decile of past capital share growth beta losers, yields insignificant results across international markets as well as even for the U.S. market only.

Overall, our findings are consistent with the fact that wealth inequality tends to increase whenever stock market returns are high (Gomez, 2017). Additionally, our line of reasoning supports empirical evidence recently reported by Zhang (2019) who shows that there exists a negative link between a firm's (option to replace) routine-based labor tasks and its exposure to systematic risk as well as its expected equity returns. Most importantly, though, our results confirm the significance of capital share growth as a source of priced risk within international equity markets.

The remainder of our study is organized as follows. Section 3.2 places our work within the current state of research and formally derives our hypotheses. Section 3.3 outlines the data set underlying our analysis and describes the methodological approach. Section 3.4 presents baseline findings and discusses the empirical evidence. Section 3.5 summarizes our findings, discusses implications, and concludes.

3.2   Related Literature and Hypothesis Development

Our study builds upon Lettau et al. (2019) who examine whether growth in the capital share of national income has explanatory power for equity characteristic portfolio returns as well as nonequity asset classes within the U.S. market. In line with Danthine and Donaldson (2002), Lettau et al. (2019) argue that wealthy people finance consumption out of asset ownership, whereas workers finance consumption out of salaries and wages. Aggregate shocks that shift capital income towards labor income are thus considered as a source of systematic risk for security holders. This tension between labor and capital has long been recognized within academia as for instance within studies by Lustig and Van Nieuwerburgh (2008) or Julliard (2007). Given this theoretical backdrop, our work adds to a broader literature stream analyzing potential interdependencies between unequal asset ownership and stock market fluctuations (Heaton and Lucas, 2000; Gomez, 2017; Guvenen, 2009; Malloy et al., 2009; Mankiw and Zeldes, 1991). More specifically, our study relates to prior academic works examining the role of redistributive shocks as a potential source of systematic risk (Danthine and Donaldson, 2002; Greenwald et al., 2014; Lettau et al., 2019).

In this regard, Heaton and Lucas (2000) present empirical evidence that income derived out of entrepreneurial ventures constitutes a source of undiversifiable risk, which in turn tends to be more highly correlated with common equity returns. Likewise, Danthine and Donaldson (2002) argue that equity returns are solely determined by the consumption and preferences of firm owners. Guvenen (2009) argues that the interaction of both, limited participation in the stock market as well as heterogeneity in the elasticity of intertemporal substitution in consumption, is relevant for macroeconomic asset pricing. Gomez (2017) finds that wealth inequality increases whenever stock market returns are high, while simultaneously arguing that higher wealth inequality predicts lower future stock returns. Greenwald et al. (2014) find that long-term stock market fluctuations are driven by shocks that redistribute production rewards between firm owners and workers.

Besides this macroeconomic asset pricing literature stream, our paper relates to a growing research field analyzing the validity and persistence of various asset pricing factors and anomalies observed within the U.S. for international markets. In this regard, prior academic work has uncovered that many patterns obtained within the U.S. deviate for international markets (Fama and French, 2012; Hou et al., 2011; Jacobs and Müller, 2018, 2020). Fama and French (2012) for instance find that Japan is an exception when it comes to the existence of the size or momentum premium. Studying 240 cross-sectional predictors, Jacobs and Müller (2018) show that there exists a large geographic heterogeneity in the significance of asset pricing factors. Relatedly, Jacobs and Müller (2020) show that the post-publication decline of asset pricing anomalies detected by McLean and Pontif (2016) for the U.S. market is not observable across a wide range of international markets. Given that prior studies to a great extent find that empirical asset pricing factors and anomalies observed within the U.S. market are not (fully) transferable to international markets, we thus hypothesize for our study as follows:

Hypothesis 1: There exists (strong) geographic heterogeneity in the explanatory power of local capital share growth for expected equity characteristic portfolio returns.

Similarly, there exists an ongoing academic debate on whether global, regional, or rather local factors are more suitable in explaining international asset prices (Griffin, 2002; Hau, 2011; Hou et al., 2011; Hollstein, 2020; Karolyi and Wu, 2014; Lewis, 2011). Throughout the past decades, national boundaries have become increasingly blurred and financial markets have become increasingly global. Thus, it is a logical endeavor to ask whether international equity returns are (increasingly) driven by global rather than local risk factors (Petzev et al., 2016). Indeed, studies conducted by Brooks and Del Negro (2005) as well as Hau (2011) underline the importance of regional and global rather than local risk factors. Karolyi and Wu (2014), however, emphasize that a partial-segmentation approach, that is a combination of global and local risk factors, is superior to purely-global and purely-local factor models.

For our study, this implies that a potential absence of explanatory power of local capital share growth for international markets might be attributable to the fact that a global capital share growth factor might be more useful in explaining international portfolio returns. Conversely, however, the bulk of most recent empirical evidence suggests that local factors are more useful in explaining international equity returns (Fama and French, 2012; Hollstein, 2020; Hou et al., 2011). For this reason, we formulate our second hypothesis as follows:

Hypothesis 2: Capital share growth is a local rather than global risk factor.

Provided that we indeed observe geographic heterogeneity in the explanatory power of capital share growth, we strive to understand potential causes of cross-country differences. Within their study, Lettau et al. (2019) argue that positive KS risk estimates are driven by imperfect risk-sharing due to unequal equity ownership. Aggregate shocks that shift capital income towards labor income are thus considered as a source of systematic risk for security holders. In this regard, it seems intuitive to assume that good news on the future growth of labor income constitutes adverse information to security holders. A security's price is determined by its future payouts (dividends). The higher a company's expenses, the smaller the amount left for potential payouts to its security holders. This is especially plausible since it is a stylized fact that labor costs represent one of the biggest cost drivers within the firm-universe. A logical conjecture thus might be that cross-country differences in unequal asset ownership lead to variations in empirical results of reported KS risk estimates. This conjecture relates to the broader literature stream arguing that limited stock market participation has an impact upon asset prices (Basak and Cuoco, 1998; Favilukis, 2013; Gomez, 2017; Guvenen, 2009; Guo, 2004). Following this line of argumentation, we further hypothesize as follows:

Hypothesis 3: Cross-country differences in the explanatory power of capital share growth are driven by variations in local wealth inequality.

However, we argue that there exist further drivers of potential cross-country differences in local capital share risk estimates. In this regard, an evident driver of cross-country variations lies in potential misreportings of a country's labor and capital share values. These figures might be distorted either via a country's aggregate income derived out of wages and salaries or a country's income obtained from the ownership of firms and financial investments. In this regard, Burq and Chancel (2020) for instance emphasize that despite improvements throughout the past decades, there still exist opaque financial systems which lack available information on income and wealth distributions across the globe. Relatedly, we argue that one of the biggest factors distorting national labor share values lies in the local shadow economy labor force. Following this line of reasoning, differences in KS risk estimates are driven by differences in national shadow economies. According to Schneider et al. (2010), the weighted average size of the shadow economy between 1999 and 2007 amounts to 36.4% within Europe and Central Asia, whereas it equals only 13.4% for high income OECD countries. These differences, in turn, impact the accuracy of estimated labor and capital shares, thus potentially explaining cross-country differences in reported KS risk estimates.

Also, and as for instance argued by Chen et al. (2011), workers' wages and salaries are particularly influenced by labor unions which simultaneously impact a firm's cost of equity. This rationale is in line with further studies in the field of labor economics as for instance the ones conducted by Abowd (1989) and Hirsch (1991). Apart from a potential increase in labor shares, these studies have uncovered that powerful labor unions reduce firms' operating flexibility, profitability, and in doing so they inevitably impact fundamental firm values. Beyond, labor unions impose a crucial burden to employment contracts in the form of wage inflexibility and workforce layoffs. Therefore, we argue that collective bargainings and trade union density increases the risk of shocks which redistribute the income between shareholders and employees. This implies that we expect capital share risk estimates to be higher within countries which exhibit higher numbers of trade unions as well as collective bargainings.

Lastly, assuming that potential shocks which redistribute the income between workers and security holders are at least partially offset by local governments, we presume a limiting effect upon KS risk estimes. As for instance argued by Alvaredo et al. (2018), a decline in public wealth limits a government's ability to redistribute income or to offset rising inequality. Also, and as for instance reported by Dominguez et al. (2012), countries which exhibit higher levels of total reserves are hypothesized to simultaneously exhibit stronger economic recovery after potential crises, thus partially offsetting adverse effects for security holders. We therefore hypothesize a negative link between a country's level of public wealth as well as a country's total reserves and reported KS risk estimates.

Overall, we lastly hypothesize as follows:

Hypothesis 4: Cross-country differences in the explanatory power of capital share growth can further be explained by differences in economic transparency, differences in the bargaining power of local workforce as well as variations in public wealth or public reserves.

3.3   Data and Methodology

3.3.1   Data Sample and Summary Statistics

To construct our final sample, we combine data from multiple sources and screen as follows. First, we derive stock market data from Datastream/Worldscope. Monthly stock returns and further stock-related measures are gathered from Datastream. Accounting data is derived from Worldscope. Equity returns are measured in U.S. dollar and winsorized at the 0.1% and 99.9% levels to account for the effect of outliers.

Second, and in order to calculate a country's capital share, we gather data on national labor shares (*labsh*) from the PENN World Table (PWT). The PWT is compiled by the University of Groningen and has served as an established source of data on real GDP across countries for over four decades. In this regard, to make local GDPs at national prices comparable across countries, international GDPs are converted to U.S. dollars (Feenstra et al., 2015). *Labsh* indicates a country's share of labor compensation in GDP at current national prices. We then calculate a country's capital share (KS) as follows: KS=1-Labsh. While Lettau et al. (2019) build their analysis on quarterly capital share growth measures, we apply annual capital share growth values due to international data availability issues. Applying annual KS data does not alter the spirit and interpretation of empirical results reported. Once applying annual KS data for the same period investigated by Lettau et al. (2019) within the U.S., we obtain values for R^2 and coefficients within the 95% confidence interval reported by Lettau et al. (2019).

We restrict our sample to countries listed in the following regional indices: MSCI North

America, MSCI Europe, MSCI Pacific, and MSCI Emerging Markets. However, if there is no data on labor share available for a certain nation, we exclude the corresponding country from our analyses. These screening criteria lead to a final sample of 45 countries within our study, including the U.S. market. Our sample period runs from January 1989 to December 2017. The start date is a tradeoff between maximizing the length of the time-series and ensuring a maximum number of countries within the study. Our end date is set by availability of data on national labor shares within the PENN World Table. Please note that while our overall sample period runs from January 1989 to December 2017, data coverage in Datastream starts later for some emerging markets. Table 3.1 exemplifies corresponding start and end dates as well as remaining summary statistics on a country-basis.

At the country-level, the average number of firms per month ranges from highest 4,444.93 (United States) to lowest 32.11 (Hungary). Average KS is highest in Qatar (0.76), Malaysia (0.67), and Egypt (0.62). Lowest average KS values are reported for Taiwan (0.29), Canada (0.33), and Switzerland (0.35). Average KS growth over one-year horizons is highest for India (1.66%), Ireland (1.52%), and Taiwan (1.12%) and lowest for Argentinia (-0.61%), Brazil (-0.46%), and Malaysia (-0.39%). Average KS growth over two-year horizons is also highest for India (3.40%), Ireland (3.05%), and Taiwan (2.26%). Lowest average KS growth values over two-year horizons accordingly are observed within Argentinia (-1.16%), Brazil (-0.91%), and Malaysia (-0.78%).

For reasons of clarity and simplicity, we cluster our chosen set of countries for the main analyses described below as follows: U.S. market, G7 + Australia (excl. U.S.)[2], and Emerging Markets[3]. Additionally, we run analyses for a World Sample, containing all applied countries with the exception of the U.S. market.

---

[2]Australia, Canada, Germany, France, Italy, Japan, and United Kingdom.
[3]Argentinia, Brazil, Chile, China, Columbia, Czech Republic, Egypt, Greece, Hungary, India, Indonesia, Malaysia, Mexico, Peru, Philippines, Poland, Qatar, Russia, South Africa, South Korea, Taiwan, Thailand, and Turkey.

Table 3.1: Summary Statistics: Data Sample and Capital Share Values

This table exemplifies summary statistics for all countries included within the analyses. Our sample period runs from M1:1989 to M12:2017, however, data coverage in Datastream starts later for some emerging markets. Columns 3 and 4 show start and end dates for each equity market correspondingly. Column 5 reports the aggregate number of firms throughout our sample period, column 6 the average number of firms per month. Column 7 states a country's worldwide percental market value as of December 2017. Column 8 shows a country's average annual KS (i.e. the percentage of national GDP at current national prices that is non-attributable to the national share of labor compensation). Columns 9 and 10 illustrate time-series averages of growth in local KS over horizons of one (H4) and two (H8) years, respectively.

(1)	(2)	(3)	(4)	(5)	(6)	(7)	(8)	(9)	(10)
Abbrev	Country	Start	End	Total # Firms	Avg # Firms/ Month	% of MV	Avg KS	Avg KS Growth (H4)	Avg KS Growth (H8)
arg	Argentinia	1/1989	12/2017	112	53.07	0.10%	0.5754	-0.61%	-1.16%
atl	Australia	1/1989	12/2017	3043	1005.39	1.94%	0.4012	0.22%	0.47%
aus	Austria	1/1989	12/2017	182	79.01	0.20%	0.4040	0.57%	1.13%
bel	Belgium	1/1989	12/2017	254	114.26	0.56%	0.3754	0.12%	0.40%
bra	Brazil	6/1994	12/2017	285	123.83	0.83%	0.4559	-0.46%	-0.91%
can	Canada	1/1989	12/2017	4743	1444.01	2.82%	0.3324	0.42%	0.68%
chi	Chile	7/1989	12/2017	253	130.27	0.35%	0.5394	0.29%	0.62%
chn	China	1/1991	12/2017	3711	1312.62	11.76%	0.4230	0.10%	0.22%
col	Columbia	1/1992	12/2017	81	38.33	0.15%	0.5204	-0.09%	-0.19%
cze	Czech Republic	6/1996	12/2017	92	29.98	0.04%	0.4870	-0.12%	-0.17%
den	Denmark	1/1989	12/2017	338	163.77	0.54%	0.3648	0.33%	0.64%
egy	Egypt	12/1997	12/2017	221	112.17	0.06%	0.6230	0.21%	0.40%
fin	Finland	1/1989	12/2017	248	107.27	0.40%	0.3987	0.81%	1.53%
fra	France	1/1989	12/2017	1737	697.22	3.49%	0.3750	-0.03%	0.12%
ger	Germany	1/1989	12/2017	1534	560.60	2.94%	0.3646	0.55%	1.15%
gre	Greece	1/1989	12/2017	396	191.45	0.07%	0.4903	-0.06%	-0.10%
hkg	Hong Kong	1/1989	12/2017	2033	779.22	4.58%	0.5027	-0.32%	-0.59%
hun	Hungary	6/1993	12/2017	75	32.11	0.04%	0.3816	0.70%	1.34%
ind	India	1/1990	12/2017	3546	1203.22	3.16%	0.4312	1.66%	3.40%
ido	Indonesia	1/1989	12/2017	641	268.68	0.68%	0.5488	-0.12%	-0.23%
ire	Ireland	1/1989	12/2017	133	54.11	0.17%	0.5157	1.52%	3.05%
ita	Italy	1/1989	12/2017	597	236.85	0.97%	0.4729	0.32%	0.69%
jap	Japan	1/1989	12/2017	5402	3045.57	8.48%	0.4265	0.17%	0.41%
mal	Malaysia	1/1989	12/2017	1311	626.35	0.61%	0.6727	-0.39%	-0.78%
mex	Mexico	1/1989	12/2017	225	93.79	0.51%	0.6102	0.37%	0.76%
net	Netherlands	1/1989	12/2017	321	142.07	0.85%	0.3918	1.05%	2.23%
nzl	New Zealand	1/1989	12/2017	254	85.97	0.13%	0.4502	0.31%	0.74%
nor	Norway	1/1989	12/2017	536	162.54	0.41%	0.4877	0.55%	0.96%
per	Peru	1/1992	12/2017	190	82.99	0.11%	0.5615	-0.12%	-0.24%
phi	Philippines	6/1989	12/2017	309	163.31	0.38%	0.5992	0.48%	0.97%
pol	Poland	6/1992	12/2017	732	240.29	0.26%	0.3983	0.59%	1.18%
por	Portugal	1/1989	12/2017	138	57.73	0.09%	0.3703	0.57%	1.18%
qat	Qatar	6/2004	12/2017	49	37.41	0.17%	0.7613	0.74%	1.49%
rus	Russia	6/1997	12/2017	547	195.74	0.84%	0.4106	0.09%	0.13%
sin	Singapore	1/1989	12/2017	1065	431.04	0.85%	0.5569	-0.11%	-0.18%
soa	South Africa	1/1989	12/2017	850	268.30	0.80%	0.4424	0.30%	0.64%
sok	South Korea	1/1989	12/2017	2672	936.82	2.24%	0.4703	0.34%	0.61%
spa	Spain	1/1989	12/2017	351	141.11	1.09%	0.3786	0.58%	1.15%
swe	Sweden	1/1989	12/2017	994	296.72	0.86%	0.4539	0.11%	0.27%
swi	Switzerland	1/1989	12/2017	407	212.19	2.12%	0.3477	0.14%	0.29%
tai	Taiwan	1/1989	12/2017	2285	870.92	1.60%	0.2882	1.12%	2.26%
tha	Thailand	1/1989	12/2017	877	371.99	0.73%	0.6107	0.18%	0.39%
tur	Turkey	1/1989	12/2017	451	190.77	0.30%	0.5913	-0.16%	-0.33%
uni	United Kingdom	1/1989	12/2017	4462	1500.34	4.51%	0.4168	-0.29%	-0.55%
usa	USA	1/1989	12/2017	11684	4444.93	35.27%	0.3909	0.22%	0.43%

3.3.2 Econometric Approach

We follow the two-step regression approach proposed by Lettau et al. (2019). It is assumed that workers do not participate in the stock market, but entirely consume their wages and salaries. Thus, worker consumption is to be neglected in the following. As in equilibrium stockholders' share of consumption is assumed to equal the capital share, stockholders' consumption is to be neglected as well (Lettau et al., 2019).

First, we run univariate time-series regressions for each of the correspodning 5x5 equity portfolios on local KS growth, indicating the growth of local capital share over horizons of one (H4) and two (H8) years:

$$R^e_{j,t+H,t} = \alpha_j + \beta_{jKS,H}\Big(\frac{KS_{t+H}}{KS_t}\Big) + u_{j,t+H,t} \tag{3.1}$$

Within equation 3.1, we use the cumulative H-period excess return on asset j from the end of t to the end of $t+H$ ($R^e_{j,t+H,t}$). In this regard, a one period portfolio return equals the quarterly portfolio return on asset j from the end of t to the end of $t+1$.

To this end, we apply the following equity characteristic portfolio sorts: 25 portfolios sorted on Size/Book-to-Market (Size/BM), Size/Investment (Size/INV), Size/Operating Profitability (Size/OP), Size/Reversal (Size/REV), Size/Momentum (Size/Mom) as well as 10 portfolios sorted on Long-Term Reversal (REV). Calculation of equity portfolio returns follow the methodology described on Kenneth French's Dartmouth website. For each of our 5x5 equity portfolios, we calculate quarterly portfolio returns in the following way:

$$1 + R_{Q,Y} = \Big(1 + \frac{R^{m1}_{Q,Y}}{100}\Big)\Big(1 + \frac{R^{m2}_{Q,Y}}{100}\Big)\Big(1 + \frac{R^{m3}_{Q,Y}}{100}\Big) \tag{3.2}$$

Equation 3.2 implies that a portfolio's return in quarter Q of year Y ($R_{Q,Y}$) is the compounded monthly return over the three months within the respective quarter. We use the quarterly 3-month T-bill rate as a proxy for the risk-free rate.

Second, we analyze whether KS risk exposures estimated within equation 3.1 ($\beta_{jKS,H}$) exhibit statistically significant explanatory power in the cross-section of average one-quarter equity portfolio returns:

$$\left(R_{j,t}^e \right) = \lambda_0 + \hat{\beta}_{j,KS,H} \lambda_{KS,H} + \epsilon_j \tag{3.3}$$

Where $R_{j,t}^e$ is the average quarterly 5x5 portfolio return and $\lambda_{KS,H}$ represents the KS risk price to be estimated within the cross-section.

The rationale beyond this two-step regression approach is to analyze whether longer-horizon (i.e. one-year and two-year) capital share risk exposures are able to explain average quarterly 5x5 equity portfolio returns. Lettau et al. (2019) argue that a more accurate estimate of KS exposure is obtained once applying longer-horizon capital share values (see Lettau et al. (2019) for detailed model specifications and justifications).

3.4 Empirical Results

3.4.1 Local Capital Share Growth in International Equity Markets

We begin the analysis by testing our first hypothesis, implying that there exists (strong) geographic heterogeneity in the explanatory power of local capital share growth for expected equity portfolio returns. In Table 3.2, we summarize baseline findings obtained from applying local KS factors to local equity portfolio returns as described in Section 3.3.2.

For comparison purposes, we show results for the U.S. market within Panel A. Panel B shows findings for G7 + Australia (excl. U.S.), Panel C for Emerging Markets, and Panel D for our World Sample (excl. U.S.).

Table 3.2: Local Capital Share Growth Across Global Equity Markets

This table shows baseline results obtained from applying growth of local capital shares (KS) to local equity portfolio returns. Reported estimates are multiplied by 100. Risk exposures are estimated following the two-step regression approach proposed by Lettau et al. (2019). First-step regression betas are estimated using country fixed-effects. Standard errors are clustered at the country-level. KS values are obtained from the 9.1 Version of the PENN World Table, accessible online at https://www.rug.nl/. Our sample period runs from M1:1989 to M12:2017. Returns are winsorized at the 0.01% and 99.9% levels. *, **, and *** indicate significance levels at the 10%, 5%, and 1% level, respectively.

	Size/BM		REV		Size/INV		Size/OP		Size/REV		Size/Mom		All Equity Portfolios	
	4	∞	4	∞	4	∞	4	∞	4	∞	4	∞	4	∞
Panel A: USA														
$\lambda_{KS,H}$	0.5095***	0.4363***	0.6769***	0.6394***	0.6964***	0.6948***	0.6227***	0.5712***	0.6833***	0.6265***	0.4468***	0.3695***	0.6059***	0.5563***
t-value	(9.18)	(9.43)	(7.63)	(7.59)	(3.27)	(5.04)	(6.30)	(8.87)	(7.75)	(8.93)	(4.75)	(4.70)	(6.48)	(7.43)
R^2	0.79	0.79	0.88	0.88	0.32	0.53	0.63	0.77	0.72	0.78	0.50	0.49	0.64	0.71
Panel B: G7 + Australia (Excl. USA)														
$\lambda_{KS,H}$	2.4072***	2.1374***	2.1004***	2.5364***	1.5884***	0.8316*	2.8828***	1.7106**	-0.5148	-1.2994*	-0.1616	-1.1883	1.3837***	0.7881
t-value	(5.79)	(2.77)	(8.09)	(5.39)	(4.03)	(1.67)	(6.39)	(2.32)	(-0.68)	(-1.91)	(-0.26)	(-1.56)	(3.89)	(1.45)
R^2	0.59	0.25	0.89	0.78	0.41	0.11	0.64	0.19	0.02	0.14	0.00	0.10	0.43	0.26
Panel C: Emerging Markets														
$\lambda_{KS,H}$	1.0112***	0.8963***	1.3274***	1.1446***	0.1222	0.0864	0.7936***	0.8498***	1.6377***	1.3407***	2.4123***	1.8317***	1.2174***	1.0249***
t-value	(5.22)	(6.22)	(5.69)	(8.00)	(0.44)	(0.36)	(2.83)	(3.57)	(6.94)	(7.35)	(6.31)	(7.49)	(4.57)	(5.50)
R^2	0.54	0.63	0.80	0.89	0.01	0.01	0.26	0.36	0.68	0.70	0.63	0.71	0.49	0.55
Panel D: World Excl. USA														
$\lambda_{KS,H}$	1.8513***	1.5574***	2.2667***	2.0845***	0.9165*	0.6218	1.4870***	1.4587***	2.3883***	2.0842***	3.8131***	3.1754***	2.1205***	1.7822***
t-value	(6.28)	(6.04)	(7.97)	(7.41)	(1.92)	(1.44)	(3.17)	(2.88)	(5.66)	(5.46)	(6.69)	(7.98)	(5.28)	(5.20)
R^2	0.63	0.61	0.88	0.87	0.14	0.08	0.30	0.27	0.58	0.56	0.66	0.73	0.53	0.52

Results for the U.S. market shown in Panel A are consistent with findings reported by Lettau et al. (2019). Across all equity portfolios, over one-year and two-year horizons, capital share growth is a highly significant priced risk factor. Even for the Size/Mom portfolios (not applied by Lettau et al. (2019)), we obtain estimates which are significant at the 1% level. Average $\lambda_{KS,H}$ values across all equity portfolio sorts within the U.S. amount to 0.6059 (t-statistics: 6.48) over one-year horizons and to 0.5563 (t-statistics: 7.42) over two-year horizons. The corresponding R^2 equals 0.64 and 0.71, respectively.

Within Panels B to D, we estimate first-step regression betas for each of our 5x5 equity portfolios using country-fixed effects. This means we calculate corresponding 5x5 equity portfolio returns as well as capital share growth values at the country level. We then append country-level portfolio returns for each of the corresponding 5x5 portfolio sorts. For instance, we append all returns obtained from lowest Size/BM portfolios (P1 of P25) for corresponding countries of each panel, accordingly. We check for robustness by applying country fixed-effects within the second, instead of first regression step following the methodology proposed by Lettau et al. (2019). Reported patterns are left unaffected, while coefficients and R^2 appear to be smaller. Corresponding standard errors are clustered at the country-level.

Within Panel B, i.e. for G7 + Australia (excl. U.S.), results indicate that capital share growth is again a significant factor in explaining equity portfolio returns. Yet, reported values are not as clear as for the U.S. market and call for a more differentiated perspective. Whereas risk estimates for Size/BM, REV, Size/INV, and Size/OP portfolios provide empirical support for capital share growth to be a priced risk factor, we obtain negative risk estimates for the Size/REV and Size/Mom portfolios (t-statistics smaller than two). Across all equity portfolios, we obtain average $\lambda_{KS,H}$ values of 1.3837 (t-statistics: 3.89) over one-year investment horizons, whereas we observe a decline to 0.7881 (t-statistics: 1.45) once applying two-year periods.

For Emerging Markets (Panel C), results imply a high explanatory power of local capital share growth for local equity portfolio returns. The only exception remains the Size/INV sort for which we observe insignificant estimates. Over one-year horizons, the average $\lambda_{KS,H}$ equals 1.2174 (t-statistics: 4.57) with an R^2 of 0.49. Unlike Panel B, the explanatory power of local capital share growth maintains for Emerging Markets over two-year investment horizons. Here, we observe an average $\lambda_{KS,H}$ of 1.0249 (t-statistics: 5.50) with a corresponding R^2 of 0.55.

Results reported for our World Sample (excluding the U.S. market) within Panel D once more corroborate the strong explanatory power of local capital share growth for international markets at an aggregate level. The pooled international results are comparable to the ones obtained for the U.S. market in statistical significance. In size, they even exceed estimes for the U.S. sample. With the exception of the Size/INV portfolio sorts, all findings are statistically significant at the 1% level. Mean $\lambda_{KS,H}$ values across all portfolio sorts amount to 2.1205 (t-statistics: 5.28) with a corresponding R^2 of 0.53 for one-year investment horizons. Considering two-year investment horizons, we observe average $\lambda_{KS,H}$ values across all portfolio sorts of 1.7822 (t-statistics: 5.20) with a corresponding R^2 of 0.52.

We interpret these results as a first affirmation of our first hypothesis, implying that capital share growth is a priced risk factor which exhibits geographic heterogeneity across international equity markets. At an aggregate level, this finding strongly supports the theory proposed by Lettau et al. (2019) that positive exposure to capital share risk yields a positive risk premium. Simultaneously, however, the empirical evidence provided in Table 3.2 implies that the capital share risk factor is unable to explain the full range of equity portfolio returns tested.

3.4.2 Local Capital Share Growth in Multi-Factor Models

We proceed by further testing our first hypothesis, implying that there exists (strong) geographic heterogeneity in the explanatory power of local capital share growth. Within their study, Lettau et al. (2019) find that $\lambda_{KS,H}$ is a strong risk factor which is able to outperform the prominent Fama-French three factor model in explaining expected returns of portfolios sorted on Size/BM within the U.S. market. Within this section, we test whether this central finding deviates for international markets. This implies that we strive to understand whether local capital share growth is an independent and robust risk factor, which contains information that is not yet covered by existing multi-factor asset pricing models within international equity markets. Otherwise, it would be reasonable to conclude that capital share growth is a simple proxy for the exposure to other, already well-known risk factors (Lettau et al., 2019).

To this end, in line with Lettau et al. (2019), we add estimated betas from alternative factor models within the cross-sectional regressions. For instance, we ordinarily estimate Fama-French three factor betas locally and then add estimated local KS risk exposure as follows:

$$\left(R_{j,t}^e\right) = \lambda_0 + \hat{\beta}_{j,KS,H}\lambda_{KS,H} + \hat{\beta}_{j,MKT}\lambda_{MKT} + \hat{\beta}_{j,SMB}\lambda_{SMB} + \hat{\beta}_{j,HML}\lambda_{HML} + \epsilon_{j,t} \quad (3.4)$$

Beyond the Fama-French three-factor model, we test for the traditional CAPM by Sharpe (1964) and Lintner (1965, 1969), the four-factor model by Carhart (1997), the five-factor model by Fama and French (2015) as well as the q-factor model proposed by Hou et al. (2015). Estimated capital share betas are calculated over two-year (H8) horizons.

In accordance with Lettau et al. (2019), we show results obtained for Size/BM portfolios for each of our chosen regions. Another reason for displaying results for the Size/BM portfolios only is that these portfolios together with portfolios sorted on long-term reversal (REV) exhibit highest statistical explanatory power of KS across all panels and time horizons as shown within Table 3.2.

Table 3.3 shows baseline findings from capital share growth as an alternative asset pricing factor in international equity markets. We start by summarizing findings for G7+Australia (excl. the U.S. market). Subsequently, we show aggregate results for Emerging Markets. Lastly, we summarize findings obtained for our World Sample (excluding the U.S. market). Our results obtained for the U.S. market imply that $\lambda_{KS,H}$ is a highly significant risk factor that almost entirely subsumes information contained in other factor model specifications. These results are consistent with findings reported by Lettau et al. (2019). For brevity reasons, we thus do not display U.S. results within Table 3.3.

Table 3.3: Capital Share Growth in Alternative Factor Models – Size/BM

This table reports cross-sectional regressions of average equity characteristic portfolio returns for 5x5 portfolios sorted on Size/BM on factor betas. Local capital share betas are estimated over horizons of two years (H8). All coefficients are multiplied by 100. Corresponding t-statistics are indicated within parentheses. Monthly returns are winsorized at the 0.01% and 99.9% levels. Our sample runs from M1:1989 to M12:2017. *, **, and *** indicate statistical significance at the 10%, 5%, and 1% level. We show results for Size/BM sorted equity portfolios only due to reasons of brevity.

	G7 + Australia (Excl. USA)					
		Panel A: CAPM				
$\lambda_{KS,H}$	$MKTRF$	SMB	HML			R^2
2.14***						0.25
(2.77)						
	-20.59***					0.44
	(-4.24)					
1.21*	-17.13***					0.51
(1.73)	(-3.38)					
		Panel B: FF 3 factors				
$\lambda_{KS,H}$	$MKTRF$	SMB	HML			R^2
	-23.05**	1.71	0.34			0.45
	(-2.10)	(1.59)	(0.16)			
1.50*	-20.19*	1.93*	-1.60			0.51
(1.64)	(-1.88)	(1.85)	(-0.68)			
		Panel C: Carhart 4 factors				
$\lambda_{KS,H}$	$MKTRF$	SMB	HML	WML		R^2
	17.10	2.88*	-1.51	-0.49		0.21
	(0.95)	(1.86)	(-0.46)	(-0.04)		
1.90**	13.45	2.22	-1.57	-1.11		0.40
(2.44)	(0.83)	(1.57)	(-0.53)	(-0.09)		
		Panel D: FF 5 factors				
$\lambda_{KS,H}$	$MKTRF$	SMB	HML	RMW	CMA	R^2
	-25.37**	0.29	0.58	-6.56	7.72	0.53
	(-1.99)	(0.20)	(0.23)	(-0.99)	(1.14)	
1.55*	-20.24	0.78	-1.91	-6.14	8.63	0.59
(1.71)	(-1.62)	(0.54)	(-0.68)	(-0.98)	(1.33)	
		Panel E: q-factors				
$\lambda_{KS,H}$	$MKTRF$	ME	IA	ROE		R^2
	-22.52*	-0.43	5.43	-3.84		0.47
	(-1.80)	(-0.10)	(0.99)	(-0.41)		
1.53*	-20.21*	-0.43	1.09	-3.83		0.54
(1.78)	(-1.69)	(-0.10)	(0.19)	(-0.43)		

Table 3 (Cont'd): Capital Share Growth in Alternative Factor Models – Size/BM

This table reports cross-sectional regressions of average equity characteristic portfolio returns for 5x5 portfolios sorted on Size/BM on factor betas. Local capital share betas are estimated over horizons of two years (H8). All coefficients are multiplied by 100. Corresponding t-statistics are indicated within parentheses. *, **, and *** indicate statistical significance at the 10%, 5%, and 1% level.

			Emerging Markets			
		Panel A: CAPM				
$\lambda_{KS,H}$	$MKTRF$	SMB	HML			R^2
0.90***						0.63
(6.22)						
	-15.79***					0.46
	(-4.43)					
0.68***	-8.17**					0.71
(4.41)	(-2.58)					
		Panel B: FF 3 factors				
$\lambda_{KS,H}$	$MKTRF$	SMB	HML			R^2
	-21.80***	0.00	4.99***			0.67
	(-3.66)	(0.00)	(3.35)			
0.56***	-17.31***	-0.41	2.39*			0.79
(3.39)	(-3.43)	(-0.54)	(1.66)			
		Panel C: Carhart 4 factors				
$\lambda_{KS,H}$	$MKTRF$	SMB	HML	WML		R^2
	-15.64**	-0.75	8.11***	-12.01***		0.77
	(-2.47)	(-0.89)	(5.52)	(-3.01)		
0.37**	-14.86**	-0.74	5.52***	-7.43*		0.81
(1.99)	(-2.51)	(-0.95)	(2.92)	(-1.69)		
		Panel D: FF 5 factors				
$\lambda_{KS,H}$	$MKTRF$	SMB	HML	RMW	CMA	R^2
	-15.69**	0.92	2.89**	-2.43	9.51***	0.77
	(-2.29)	(1.16)	(1.96)	(-0.59)	(2.98)	
0.39**	-14.77**	0.47	1.80	0.34	7.25**	0.81
(2.04)	(-2.32)	(0.61)	(1.23)	(0.09)	(2.30)	
		Panel E: q-factors				
$\lambda_{KS,H}$	$MKTRF$	ME	IA	ROE		R^2
	-8.26	-0.42	1.65	-17.28***		0.75
	(-1.54)	(-0.33)	(0.51)	(-4.55)		
0.3836	-9.62*	-0.80	2.05	-11.05**		0.78
(1.58)	(-1.84)	(-0.64)	(0.65)	(-2.05)		

Table 3 (Cont'd): Capital Share Growth in Alternative Factor Models – Size/BM

This table reports cross-sectional regressions of average equity characteristic portfolio returns for 5x5 portfolios sorted on Size/BM on factor betas. Local capital share betas are estimated over horizons of two years (H8). All coefficients are multiplied by 100. Corresponding t-statistics are indicated within parentheses. *, **, and *** indicate statistical significance at the 10%, 5%, and 1% level.

		World (Excl. USA)				
		Panel A: CAPM				
$\lambda_{KS,H}$	$MKTRF$					R^2
1.56***						0.61
(6.04)						
	-13.44***					0.43
	(-4.19)					
1.20***	-6.57**					0.68
(4.18)	(-2.13)					
		Panel B: Fama/French 3 factors				
$\lambda_{KS,H}$	$MKTRF$	SMB	HML			R^2
	-24.29***	-0.30	3.38**			0.64
	(-4.04)	(-0.34)	(2.49)			
1.12***	-20.09***	-1.03	1.01			0.80
(4.08)	(-4.30)	(-1.50)	(0.86)			
		Panel C: Carhart 4 factors				
$\lambda_{KS,H}$	$MKTRF$	SMB	HML	WML		R^2
	-22.76***	-0.51	6.04***	-8.78		0.63
	(-3.06)	(-0.53)	(2.98)	(-1.20)		
1.13***	-20.73***	-1.19	2.72	-4.26		0.79
(3.84)	(-3.60)	(-1.55)	(1.53)	(-0.74)		
		Panel D: Fama/French 5 factors				
$\lambda_{KS,H}$	$MKTRF$	SMB	HML	RMW	CMA	R^2
	-14.39**	0.92	0.40	0.46	18.58***	0.82
	(-2.46)	(1.38)	(0.31)	(0.11)	(4.44)	
0.66**	-15.49***	0.30	-0.28	2.50	13.85***	0.85
(2.16)	(-2.88)	(0.44)	(-0.23)	(0.60)	(3.14)	
		Panel E: q-factors				
$\lambda_{KS,H}$	$MKTRF$	ME	IA	ROE		R^2
	-13.49**	-2.81**	5.17	-20.52***		0.73
	(-2.26)	(-2.03)	(1.51)	(-3.88)		
1.03***	-16.34***	-3.22***	4.98*	-0.14*		0.84
(3.58)	(-3.41)	(-2.92)	(1.84)	(-1.74)		

As shown within Table 3.3, the explanatory power of $\lambda_{KS,H}$ for G7+Australia (excl. U.S.) is substantially reduced once adding alternative factor betas. While being initially significant at the 1% level (t-statistics: 2.77) over one-year horizons, the KS risk estimate is left only marginally relevant (t-statistics smaller than two) within four out of five alternative model specifications. The only exception remains the Carhart four-factor model (Panel C). Here, $\lambda_{KS,H}$ remains significant at the 5% level (t-statistics: 2.44). This finding implies that, unlike the U.S. market, the information contained within $\lambda_{KS,H}$ is almost entirely subsumed by alternative factors. This pattern also holds for portfolios sorted on long-term reversal (REV) as well as all other equity portfolio sorts. Even if having statistically significant explanatory power for certain equity characteristic portfolio groups, the information contained within the capital share factor seems to be almost entirely subsumed by existing factor specifications.

For Emerging Markets, our results shown in Table 3.3 imply that the information of KS risk estimates is not subsumed by alternative factor betas but rather adds additional explanatory power to these model specifications. Once adding the capital share factor, $\lambda_{KS,H}$ remains statistically significant at the 5%-level across four out of five alternative factor model specifications. For instance, cross-sectional R^2 increases from 0.46 to 0.71 once adding $\lambda_{KS,H}$ to the CAPM, whereas the KS factor alone explains roughly 63% in the cross-section. This pattern also holds for other equity characteristic portfolio returns within Emerging Markets (not shown for brevity issues).

Similar to Emerging Markets, we find that adding $\lambda_{KS,H}$ as a risk factor increases cross-sectional R^2 across all equities for our World Sample. Wihtin four out of five factor model specifications, $\lambda_{KS,H}$ remains even relevant at the 1% level in explaining cross-sectional portfolio returns. Unlike the U.S. market, though, the information contained within capital share growth does not subsume the information contained within other factors in international equity markets.

Taken together, we interpret our results reported in Tables 3.2 and 3.3 as a clear affirmation of our first hypothesis implying that there exists (strong) geographic heterogeneity in the explanatory power of local capital share growth for expected equity characteristic portfolio returns.

3.4.3   Global Capital Share Growth in International Equity Markets

We continue the analysis by testing our second hypothesis, implying that capital share growth is a local rather than global risk factor in a quest to further analyze the existence of and potential causes for international market segmentations. To construct a global KS factor, we apply market capitalization-weighted annual capital share values of our full set of applied countries (including the U.S.). For analyses described below, we again follow the two-step regression approach by Lettau et al. (2019). In line with Section 3.4.1, we estimate first-step regression betas for each of our 5x5 equity portfolios using country-fixed effects. Reported results are, however, robust to applying country fixed-effects within the second rather than first regression step following the methodology proposed by Lettau et al. (2019).

Table 3.4 summarizes corresponding findings. Panel A reports findings for the U.S. market. Panel B summarizes the empirical evidence for G7 + Australia (excluding the U.S. market). Panel C shows results for Emerging Markets. Finally, Panel D presents insights for our World Sample (excluding the U.S. market).

Results within Panel A indicate that our global KS factor is statistically significant in explaining U.S. equity portfolio returns. While results for one-year investment horizons remain statistically significant, they are, however, in part substantially reduced. Over two-year investment horizons, U.S. results seem to change only slightly. An exception remains the Size/Mom portfolio which increases in both, size and significance, over one and two-year investment perspectives.

Table 3.4: Global Capital Share Growth Across Global Equity Markets

This table shows baseline results obtained from applying growth of global capital shares (KS) to local equity portfolio returns. To construct a global KS factor, we apply market capitalization-weighted annual capital share values of our full set of applied countries (including the U.S.). Reported estimates are multiplied by 100. Risk exposures are estimated following the two-step regression approach proposed by Lettau et al. (2019). First-step regression betas are estimated using country fixed-effects. Standard errors are clustered at the country-level. KS values are obtained from the 9.1 Version of the PENN World Table, accessible online at https://www.rug.nl/. Our sample period runs from M1:1989 to M12:2017. Returns are winsorized at the 0.01% and 99.9% levels. *, **, and *** indicate significance levels at the 10%, 5%, and 1% level, respectively.

	Size/BM		REV		Size/INV		Size/OP		Size/REV		Size/Mom		All Equity Portfolios	
	4	8	4	8	4	8	4	8	4	8	4	8	4	8
Panel A: USA														
$\lambda_{KS,H}$	0.4331***	0.2944***	1.1611**	0.6252***	0.5561**	0.4908***	0.5301***	0.3719***	0.7121***	0.4850***	0.7954***	0.3789***	0.6980***	0.4410***
t-value	(7.49)	(9.64)	(1.97)	(7.70)	(2.66)	(6.05)	(7.23)	(9.95)	(3.91)	(8.42)	(8.34)	(7.32)	(5.26)	(8.18)
R^2	0.71	0.80	0.33	0.88	0.24	0.61	0.69	0.81	0.40	0.76	0.75	0.70	0.52	0.76
Panel B: G7 + Australia (Excl. USA)														
$\lambda_{KS,H}$	0.5966***	0.5781***	0.7566	0.6333	0.7809***	0.6225***	1.0240***	0.9029***	-0.2603	0.3880	0.1168	0.4602	0.5039**	0.5975**
t-value	(3.79)	(3.93)	(1.36)	(1.30)	(4.28)	(4.09)	(3.79)	(4.04)	(-0.60)	(1.00)	(0.45)	(1.39)	(2.18)	(2.63)
R^2	0.39	0.40	0.19	0.18	0.44	0.42	0.38	0.42	0.02	0.04	0.01	0.08	0.24	0.26
Panel C: Emerging Markets														
$\lambda_{KS,H}$	0.3472***	0.1837*	0.4538	0.1919	0.2263	0.2956	0.1094	0.093	-0.0386	-0.0027	-0.0527	-0.1400	0.1742	0.1036
t-value	(2.74)	(1.89)	(1.30)	(0.64)	(1.10)	(1.42)	(0.56)	(0.60)	(-0.17)	(-0.02)	(-0.34)	(-0.83)	(0.87)	(0.62)
R^2	0.25	0.13	0.17	0.05	0.05	0.08	0.01	0.02	0.00	0.00	0.01	0.03	0.08	0.05
Panel D: World Excl. USA														
$\lambda_{KS,H}$	0.3473**	0.2563**	0.8482**	0.5829*	0.3776	0.3873	0.3115	0.3654	-0.1304	0.0157	0.0529	0.0078	0.3012	0.2992
t-value	(2.59)	(2.09)	(2.46)	(1.81)	(1.35)	(1.39)	(1.06)	(1.49)	(-0.39)	(0.06)	(0.28)	(0.03)	(1.23)	(1.15)
R^2	0.23	0.16	0.43	0.29	0.07	0.08	0.05	0.09	0.01	0.00	0.00	0.00	0.13	0.10

Similar to the U.S. market, we observe for G7 + Australia (excl. U.S.), shown in Panel B, that our global risk factor is able to explain a large fraction of expected equity portfolio returns. Consistent with results reported in Table 3.2, however, the global factor is unable to explain expected returns of portfolios sorted on Size/REV as well as of portfolios sorted on Size/Mom. Across all equity portfolio sorts the global KS risk estimate amounts to 0.5039 (t-statistics: 2.18) with a corresponding R^2 of 0.24 over one-year horizons. Accordingly, over two-year horizons we report an average $\lambda_{KS,II}$ of 0.5975 (t-statistics: 2.63) and a corresponding R^2 of 0.26.

Conversely, as further shown within Table 3.4, the explanatory power of capital share growth decreases considerably once applying a global rather than local risk factor for Panels C and D. At an aggregate level (average values across all equity portfolio sorts), results for Emerging Markets (Panel C) as well as our World Sample (Panel D) become insignificant. These findings underpin our hypothesis that capital share growth is a local risk factor. Therefore, our findings are in line with studies by Fama and French (2012), Hollstein (2020) as well as Hou et al. (2011) who emphasize the importance of local factors in explaining expected returns across international markets.

3.4.4 Cross-Country Analyses: Determinants of Capital Share Risk Estimates

3.4.4.1 Country Characteristics

An important aspect in empirical asset pricing is to understand why risk factors matter within certain countries while they are irrelevant within other countries. In this section, we thus strive to understand and test potential drivers of global differences in reported capital share risk estimates. In accordance with our third and forth hypotheses derived and outlined in Section 3.2 as well as prior cross-country studies, we identify the following set of variables described below. Detailed variable definitions and data sources are given in Appendix B of the Electronic Supplementary Material.

First, and in order to test for the theoretical explanation given by Lettau et al. (2019), we apply multiple variables to account for cross-country differences in private wealth inequality. Our first proxy is a country's domestic investor participation rate. This figure stands for the fraction of domestic households holding directly stocks in the domestic stock market and is taken from Barniv et al. (2010) in accordance with Giannetti and Koskinen (2010). Further, we account for a country's top 1% and bottom 50% income shares. The logic behind inclusion of these two variables is that Lettau et al. (2019) hypothesize a positive relationship between the top 1% income share and corresponding capital share values. Relatedly, we test for a potential negative link between a country's bottom 50% income share and corresponding capital share values. The fourth proxy illustrates the average of a country's private financial assets. Lastly, we include the portion of local population that is covered by at least one social protection benefit as we consider social protection benefits to partially offset implications of private wealth inequality.

Second, we apply a set of four variables to account for a country's overall economic opaqueness: An inequality transparency index, the average size of local shadow economies, an opacity index, and the number of news articles per country. The wealth inequality transparency index is gathered from the World Inequality Database accessible online at https://wid.world and measures the availability as well as quality of information on wealth inequality across countries. The average size of local shadow economies is a measure taken from Schneider et al. (2010), indicating the average size of national shadow economies in percent of official GDP. The opacity index is a proxy for lcoal information opaqueness which we gather from Kurtzman et al. (2004). It measures the extent to which a country lacks clear and accurate as well as widely accepted business practices among firms, investors and governments. Lastly, the number of news articles is taken from Griffin et al. (2011) and stands for the number of news articles scaled by the number of firms per country.

Third, to account for the bargaining power of workers and employees, we include the following proxies which we obtain from the International Labour Organisation (ILO): Collective bargaining, trade union density as well as the number of days not worked by 1,000 workers. Collective bargaining stands for the fraction of employees covered by one or more collective agreement. Trade union density indicates the number of union members who are employees as a percentage of the total number of employees. Finally, we apply the number of days not worked because of strike per 1,000 workers. As outlined within Section 3.2, the rationale beyond inclusion of these three proxies is that we hypothesize that collective bargaining as well as trade unions increase the risk of potential shocks which redistribute the income between shareholders and employees.

Lastly, we include two proxies for differences in public wealth and public reserves: Total Nonfinancial Government Assets as well as Total Reserves by GDP. The first variable comprises produced assets as for instance buildings and inventories as well as nonproduced assets such as natural resources (e.g. oil or gas). The latter comprises the holdings of monetary gold, special drawing rights, reserves of IMF members held by the IMF as well as holdings of foreign exchange which are controlled by monetary authorities.

3.4.4.2 Cross-Sectional Regressions

To analyze the relationship between obtained capital share risk estimates and our chosen set of country variables, we perform various cross-sectional regression specifications. In the regression analyses below, our dependent variable constitutes the average capital share risk estimate $\lambda_{KS,H}$ across applied equity characteristic portfolio sorts as reported within the last column of Table 3.2.

Our chosen set of country characteristics reported in Section 3.4.4.1 primarily exhibits a panel data structure. Occasionally, however, they only exhibit the country-dimension, implying that they are time-invariant. Thus, we apply averages of time-series country variables and exclusively apply cross-sectional regressions below. In doing so, we are able to analyze drivers of differences in cross-country capital share growth risk estimates.

Table 3.5 reports empirical results for various cross-sectional regression specifications.

Table 3.5: Cross-Country Analyses of Average KS Risk Estimates

This table shows results of cross-sectional regressions examining the significance of our chosen set of country variables. The dependent variable is the within-country time-series average estimate of two-year capital share growth risk estimates as reported within Table 2. Reported estimates are multiplied by 100. t-statistics are shown within parentheses. *, **, and *** indicate statistical significance at the 10%, 5% as well as 1% level.

	M1	M2	M3	M4	M5	M6	M7	M8	M9	M10	M11	M12	M13	M14
	Dependent Variable: Average two-year KS risk estimates (H8)													
Investor Participation Rate	-0.06834 (-0.11)													
Top 1% Income Share		0.39343 (0.51)												
Bottom 50% Income Share			-0.42393 (-0.56)											
Net Private Financial Wealth				-0.97800* (-1.75)										
Social Security Coverage					-0.00431* (-1.88)									
Wealth Transparency Index						0.01223 (0.65)								
Shadow Economy							-0.00264 (-0.72)							
Opacity Index								-0.0418 (-0.91)						
Number of News Articles									0.00269* (1.79)					
Collective Bargaining										-0.00048 (-0.34)				
Trade Union Density											-0.00053 (-0.22)			
Days not Worked by 1,000 Workers												0.0028 (1.23)		
Nonfinancial Government Assets													-0.00123* (-1.79)	
Total Reserves by GDP														-0.51884*** (-2.10)
R^2	0.00	0.01	0.01	0.15	0.10	0.01	0.01	0.03	0.10	0.00	0.00	0.07	0.14	0.10

As illustrated within Table 3.5, our chosen set of proxies for economic opaqueness as well as relative bargaining strength of local workforce are insignificant in explaining cross-country differences in average capital share growth risk estimates, with the exception of a country's number of news articles. This proxy, which is significant at the 10% level, implies that there exists a positive link between the number of news articles and a country's average capital share risk estimates.

Conversely, though, two of our chosen variables to proxy for wealth inequality are significant at the 10% level: Net private financial wealth as well as social security coverage. These variables are however inversely related to a country's average KS risk estimates. This finding underpins the theoretical backdrop given by Lettau et al. (2019) in an international setting: The smaller the level of private wealth inequality, the lower the amount of capital market risk beard by a small subset of investors, thus the lower the expected compensation in terms of equity portfolio returns. The insignificance of the proxy for (domestic) investor participation rate does not contradict this rationale. For instance, while the investor participation rate within the U.S. is among the highest worldwide, most households who participate in the stock market own very little stocks (Lettau et al., 2019). That is, the participation rate itself does not give information about the level of risk-sharing prevalent in the equity market.

Further, reported results shown in Table 3.5 illustrate the significance of our proxies for differences in public wealth and public reserves. The variable *Total Nonfinancial Government Assets* is significant at the 10% level, whereas the proxy *Total Reserves by GDP* is significant at the 5% level in explaining cross-country differences in average KS risk estimates. This finding is in accordance with the theoretical motivation taken from Alvaredo et al. (2018), implying that a decline in public wealth is associated with a decline in the government's ability to redistribute income or to offset rising inequality. Beyond, this finding is in line with empirical evidence reported by Dominguez et al. (2012) who illustrate that countries which exhibit higher levels of total reserves are found to simultaneously exhibit stronger economic recovery after the global financial crisis, thus partially offsetting adverse effects for security holders.

Overall, we interpret results shown within Table 3.5 as an affirmation of our third hypothesis, implying that cross-country differences in the explanatory power of capital share growth are driven by variations in local wealth inequality. Simultaneously, however, we discard our fourth hypothesis as the only significant variables remain the number of news articles scaled by the number of firms within a country as well as those variables proxying for differences in public wealth as well as public reserves. Conversely, proxies applied for the relative bargaining strength of local workforce as well as the majority of variables included to account for economic opaqueness are not able to explain cross-country differences in KS risk estimates.

3.4.5   Cross-Country Trading Strategy

Can we exploit the information contained within capital share growth by a simple trading strategy? To this point, reported capital share risk estimates are entirely based upon in-sample calculations. To assess the relative importance and robustness of the capital share growth factor, we thus proceed by constructing an out-of-sample investment strategy. Specifically, we perform rolling ten-year-window regressions of cumulative quarterly equity characteristic portfolio returns on local capital share growth for each portfolio style (5x5 Size/BM portfolios, 10 REV portfolios, 5x5 Size/INV portfolios, 5x5 Size/OP portfolios, 5x5 Size/REV portfolios, 5x5 Size/Mom portfolios), on a country-basis. This procedure is consistent with the methodological approach described in Section 3.3.2, with the exception that we now conduct country estimates. In a next step, we go long the decile of past capital share growth beta winners and short the decile of past capital share growth beta losers for the following investment quarter.

Table 3.6 summarizes average quarterly long-short returns. Additionally, we report corresponding sharpe ratios, quarterly minimum returns, and standard deviations. Investment strategies are built for the U.S. market only, G7 + Australia (excl. the U.S.), Emerging Markets as well as for a World Sample (excl. the U.S.) and across the full range of applied countries. Panel A shows findings when applying one-year horizons for cumulative portfolio returns as well as capital share growth estimates. Panel B summarizes findings for two-year horizons.

Table 3.6: Out-of-Sample Long-Short Portfolio Returns

This table reports portfolio returns obtained from long-short investment strategies based upon local capital share growth betas (first step regression beta as described by Lettau et al. (2019)). We perform rolling ten-year-window regressions of cumulative quarterly equity characteristic portfolio returns on local capital share growth for each portfolio style (5x5 Size/BM portfolios, 10 REV portfolios, 5x5 Size/INV portfolios, 5x5 Size/OP portfolios, 5x5 Size/REV portfolios, 5x5 Size/Mom portfolios), for each country, respectively. In a next step, we go long the decile of past capital share growth beta winners and short the decile of past capital share growth beta losers for the following investment quarter. Returns are winsorized at the 0.01% and 99.9% levels. The sample runs from M1:1989 to M12:2017.

Panel A: One-Year Capital Share Growth (H4)				
	ret quarterly	sharpe ratio	min ret	sd
USA	3.13% (1.22)	0.27	-7.72%	11.48%
G7 + Australia (Excl. USA)	0.96% (0.35)	0.08	-19.51%	12.31%
Emerging Markets	-1.10% (-0.29)	-0.06	-45.34%	17.09%
World Excl. USA	-0.19% (-0.10)	-0.02	-17.94%	8.43%
World Incl. USA	-0.16% (-0.09)	-0.02	-18.03%	8.41%
Panel B: Two-Year Capital Share Growth (H8)				
	ret quarterly	sharpe ratio	min ret	sd
USA	1.06% (0.36)	0.08	-37.58%	13.30%
G7 + Australia (Excl. USA)	-1.53% (-0.53)	-0.12	-19.29%	12.96%
Emerging Markets	-2.39% (-0.54)	-0.12	-67.76%	19.81%
World Excl. USA	0.44% (0.26)	0.06	-12.83%	7.48%
World Incl. USA	0.51% (0.30)	0.07	-13.99%	7.48%

As shown within Table 3.6, returns obtained from our out-of-sample investment strategy illustrate that investors are not able to exploit information from this single capital share growth factor in real time. Across all regions, even within the U.S. market, our strategy yields insignificant quarterly portfolio return estimates. This finding holds for both, one-year and two-year capital share growth estimates. Our results simultaneously show that sharpe ratios are below the critical value of one while minimum returns and standard deviations are considerably high.

At an aggregate level, this finding exemplifies that - while exhibiting great in-sample explanatory power and significance - the information contained in the capital share growth factor seems difficult to be exploited out-of-sample.

3.5   Conclusion

Our study analyzes whether growth in the capital share (KS) of aggregate income (GDP) can explain equity portfolio returns in international stock markets as proposed by Lettau et al. (2019) for the U.S. market.

Reported results imply that local capital share growth is a priced risk factor across international markets. There exists, however, strong geographic heterogeneity in the explanatory power of this risk factor. Applying country fixed-effects regressions, we find that capital share growth has particularly high explanatory power for equity returns obtained within the United States as well as within Emerging Markets. Unlike the U.S. market, though, the information contained in the KS risk factor of Emerging Markets does not subsume information contained in alternative factor models as for instance the Fama-French three factor or q-factor models, but rather adds additional explanatory content to these model specifications. For G7 + Australia (excl. U.S.), we find that even if having statistically significant explanatory power for certain equity characteristic portfolio groups, the information contained within the capital share factor seems to be almost entirely subsumed by existing factor model specifications.

Furthermore, our results imply that capital share growth is a local, rather than global risk factor. Once applying global capital share growth estimates, the explanatory power of this factor either disappears entirely or is at least substantially reduced. Beyond, cross-sectional regression analysis reveals that country differences in KS risk estimates can best be explained by cross-country variations in private wealth inequality as well as country-differences in public wealth/reserves. Simultaneously, we report that proxies for economic opaqueness as well as relative bargaining strength of local workforce are primarily insignificant in explaining cross-country differences in average capital share growth risk estimates.

Finally, we are able to illustrate that - while exhibiting great in-sample explanatory power and significance - the information contained in the capital share growth factor seems difficult to be exploited out-of-sample. An investment strategy that goes long the decile of past capital share growth beta winners and short the decile of past capital share growth beta losers, yields insignificant results across international markets as well as even for the U.S. market only.

Chapter 4

The Pricing of European Non-Performing Real Estate Loan Portfolios

This chapter presents the third dissertation study which focuses on stock market reactions of European vendor banks to distressed loan sale announcements.

_____

Zusatzmaterial online
Zusätzliche Informationen sind in der Online-Version dieses Kapitel (https://doi.org/10.1007/978-3-658-35479-4_4) enthalten.

4.1   Introduction

Non-performing loans (NPL), commonly referred to as loans in arrears for at least 90 days, have continuously been characterized as the top priority of the European Central Bank (ECB) and continue to attract central attention (ECB, 2018a,b). With the outbreak of the European debt crisis, the quality of banks' assets had deteriorated in a manner that, despite robust economic recovery and a variety of regulatory efforts, NPL still today pose a threat to bank and thrift institutions. Against this backdrop, the European regulator requires banks to develop effective strategies for reducing NPL, to set up clear governance and to operate powerful work-out structures (ECB, 2017). The ECB assists with a variety of guidance measures, and especially since 2014, one of the core advices is active portfolio reduction, effectively requiring banks to sell or securitize their (mostly real estate based) residual claims on NPL holdings to loan investors in the secondary market.

With the divestiture of NPL, risky and complex bank assets are transferred from a bank-based to a market-based financial system, which raises a number of critical pricing issues. In order to establish a stable secondary market environment for distressed assets in the long term, efficient loan portfolio pricings and fair compensations of the given risk-return profiles are necessary. The subprime crisis of the last decade, however, revealed severe problems of global capital markets in the evaluation of related structured real estate finance products like collateralized loan obligations and similar asset backed securities. Woltering et al. (2018) detect equity mispricing of property-holding companies in 11 countries during 2005 to 2014, which can be exploited using simple trading strategies based on net asset value spreads. Gallo et al. (2000), Mori and Ziobrowski (2011) and Cici et al. (2011) provide additional evidence in favor of equity mispricing in the case of U.S. REITs.

In equity capital markets, shareholders act as claimants of a company's residual income which is very close to the bank lender's position in distressed loan assets. Debt capital markets, on the contrary, are less liquid in comparison and potential buyers of loan portfolios are required to spend significant effort on a precise NPL evaluation. In this context, Demirgüç-Kunt and Levine (2004) analyze pricing issues with respect to accounting-based valuations of interest-bearing assets by comparing bank-based and market-based financial systems in the aftermath of financial crises. They report evidence that institutions in bank-based systems tend to postpone necessary balance sheet restructurings in order to delay the effects of losses, whereas this option is not available for investors in market-based financial systems.

If the market-based system provides superior valuation skills, the pricing of loan portfolios should mostly profit when the heterogeneity and individuality of the underlying assets is as large as in the case of real estate collateral. The NPL sale should reduce outsider uncertainty on banks' asset values and raise confidence in their balance sheet statements. Additionally, with the sale of a loan portfolio, the bank's management signals that it does not perceive a significantly higher evaluation as compared to investors in the secondary market. Otherwise, the transaction parties would not concede on a purchase price, which effectively clears the market. In analogy, the NPL divestiture announcement can be interpreted as a signaling from the bank's management that it is not overconfident with respect to the proceeds from their NPL portfolios. Given that residual value exists, NPL sales recover (regulatory) liquidity immediately and transfer the risks and work-out expenses to the transferee (Irani and Meisenzahl, 2017).

While NPL sales increased significantly over the last years, there is only scarce evidence on market values of debt and NPL portfolios (see Section 4.2). These are depleted into secondary markets that are less liquid and market participants take time and effort to evaluate the respective assets. As most of the banks associated with NPL divestiture activity in Europe are exchange-listed, the stock market reaction to the announcement of the sales also indicates to some degree whether the realized sales prices are generally perceived as adequate. Additionally, the sales execution by itself reduces the uncertainty on the value of current risky bank assets which brings us to expect a positive share price reaction on the announcement of NPL deals. Given the ECB pressure on banks to dispose of NPL, we assume that the regulator expects the same effect.

In addition, the window of opportunity to transfer assets under distress is narrowing, as the determination of NPL is strongly linked to macroeconomic and bank-specific factors. A number of studies expect NPL to increase during potential economic downturns (Dimitrios et al., 2016; Keeton and Morris, 1987; Klein, 2013; Louzis et al., 2012), inducing a supply shock for this kind of portfolios. The level of price response should depend on the level of uncertainty resolved, the specific situation of the selling bank and the quality of the buyers or the appreciation of the buyer's competence. Therefore, we expect a) particularly positive effects in real estate deals, b) significant explanations by bank-specific factors and c) sales of real estate assets to be particularly connected to specialized financial investors.

The aim of this paper is to anticipate how complex asset sales whose cash flows are heavily dependent on real estate income are evaluated by capital market participants. This work provides both banks' decision makers and regulators with an indication how the cleaning of balance sheets from distressed assets will result in revaluations of bank equity. We synthesize a unique transaction database with 476 NPL sales for the period 2012 to 2018. As a starting point, we clarify descriptive statistics of the European NPL market, which so far lacks transparency and publicly available basic information on portfolio size and components. In particular, we are curious to understand the role of real estate in these transactions and the relevant market participants regarding real estate NPL deals. We find that about two thirds of transactions are directly related to real estate collateral. Considering mixed loan pool portfolio sales, where real estate collateral is involved in unknown proportions, this majority further increases (app. 90%). Thus, the pricing of NPL sales is largely determined by the underlying rental income and potential property proceedings in the real estate market to cover loan claims of the debtor. Second, using traditional event study methodology, we empirically analyze valuation effects of 317 distressed loan sale announcements at European banking institutions during the period 2012 to 2018, both generally and with a special focus on real estate collateral. Third, given significant valuation effects, we want to understand whether the effects can be explained by bank-specific characteristics of the vendor or specific characteristics of the sold NPL portfolios, such as the nature of collateral and (relative) portfolio size.

The analysis is structured as follows. Section 4.2 provides a literature overview and formally derives our hypotheses. Section 4.3 describes data synthesis and the methodology for the empirical part of the analysis. This includes a structural assessment of NPL market descriptive statistics. Section 4.4 presents empirical evidence on NPL sale announcement effects and critically discusses the results. Finally, Section 4.5 concludes with a summary and implications of this work.

4.2   Related Literature and Hypothesis Development

The capital market based evaluation of various corporate actions like acquisitions and divestitures has traditionally been examined with event study methodology (Binder, 1998; MacKinlay, 1997). We connect our research to a number of studies that analyze market feedback following divestiture announcements of firms that sell non-performing (Brown et al., 1994; Lasfer et al., 1996) or non-core (Comment and Jarrell, 1995; John and Ofek, 1995) assets. This strand of literature generally reports positive feedback from the stock market and interprets this result as adjustment for the distress cost reduction (Lasfer et al., 1996) and reversal of value-destroying diversification (Clubb and Stouraitis, 2002).

In the literature stream that examines loan announcements, James (1987) reports positive stock returns of borrowers to the announcement of large new bank loan agreements. Maskara and Mullineaux (2011) and Huang et al. (2012) also focus on borrower stock returns related to large loan announcements, where sizeable information asymmetries are presented. Gande and Saunders (2012) suggest that loan sales generate moral hazard problems for banks that could potentially retain higher quality assets or convey sensitive (negative) information about borrowers (Gande and Saunders, 2012; Pennacchi, 1988). Dahiya et al. (2003) conduct the first series of tests with loans under distress (pp. 153). Based on a small sample of U.S. borrowers between 1995 and 1998 ($n=29$), including a sub-panel ($n=15$) of subpar loans, they obtain negative but insignificant results for the vendor.

We find several indications, albeit outside of the journal literature, that these findings could be transferable to banks that announce (divestiture) information about (real estate based) loan and mortgage portfolios. Dick (2010) analyzes NPL transactions from three European countries ($n=38$) for the timespan 2003 to 2007 and documents neutral evidence. Geiger et al. (2007) analyze European NPL portfolio sales ($n=56$) with real estate collateral during 1990 to 2005 and find significant positive stock market reactions for the loan announcements with worst credit quality and small negative significant effects for loan portfolios with better credit quality. Gentgen (2007) investigates NPL transactions from Aareal Bank ($n=4$) during the period 2005 to 2007 in Germany with inconsistent results. More recently, Faa (2019) reports significant and positive announcement effects for NPL sales at Italian banks during the period 2013 to 2019 ($n=63$).

All in all, the empirical evidence from prior literature is broad but inconclusive. None of the earlier studies was able to synthesize large sample sizes across different asset classes, countries and longer time-spans simultaneously. Research in the banking literature yields a number of arguments in favor of a positive market reaction following NPL divestiture. There is evidence that banks are generally incentivized to sell loans to meet (short-term) liquidity needs under the new Basel III regime, either by raising capital or reducing the amount of risk-weighted assets (Boudriga et al., 2009; Irani and Meisenzahl, 2017). As a consequence, bank capitalization is altered in favor of the capital adequacy ratio, adjusting banks' balance sheets in favor of the security holder (Kwan and Eisenbeis, 1997). Considering that failing banks generally report significant proportions of NPL prior to failure or distress (Berger and DeYoung, 1997; Jin et al., 2011), selling risky assets may also be interpreted as a signaling to the equity market about the vendor's willingness to ensure smooth functioning after negative shocks (Granja et al., 2017), while banks continue to operate under increased regulatory pressure (ECB, 2018a,b). In addition, NPL sales should reduce the bank's complexity, transfer the future management costs to the transferee and help to increase financial stability (Krause et al., 2017; Irani and Meisenzahl, 2017). Thus, we first hypothesize:

Hypothesis 1: Announcements of NPL divestiture activity coincide with significant positive valuation effects, as measured by the cumulative abnormal returns of the vendor share price.

Given the current market characteristics in the European NPL market (see Section 4.3.1), the pricing of NPL portfolios is largely defined by expected rental income and potential property sale proceeds in the real estate market to cover the debtors' loan claims. Real estate generally demands a highly distinct skillset to adequately manage important features of collateral, as it is characterized by its immobility, heterogeneity, complexity and indivisibility (Breuer and Nadler, 2012)). Yet, its tangibility gives both vendor and the acquirer the opportunity to estimate its intrinsic value and facilitates the evaluation compared to the appraisal of corporate or unsecured consumer debt. Based on this tangibility, the bidding price on real estate loans should likely be higher compared to other types of collateral. This should, in turn, affect the revaluation of bank capitalization in excess, ultimately inducing banks to carry less risk (Berger and DeYoung, 1997; Salas and Saurina, 2002). In the literature that analyzes NPL determinants at the loan level, a number of studies have started to account for real estate separately, the results yielding a further indication about the distinct features (Adelino et al., 2016; Beck et al., 2015; Ghosh, 2015). For these reasons, we hypothesize an appraisal difference depending on collateral quality, expressed in the net effect of distinct real estate attributes:

Hypothesis 2: Due to its distinct features, the sale of real estate NPL is reflected in excess significant positive cumulative abnormal returns of the vendor, as compared to the overall cumulative abnormal return of vendor banks.

Given that significant valuation effects may in fact be observed, another question arising is whether, and if so how, these abnormal returns can be explained upon the basis of vendor characteristics. This question is particularly appealing for both, investors and regulators alike. Investors might target those banks having the highest likelihood in generating abnormal returns. Regulators might adjust their guidance accordingly. Prior research has widely acknowledged the interlinkage between a bank's amount of NPL and its insolvency risk (Arena and Yan, 2008; Berger and DeYoung, 1997; Jin et al., 2011; Whalen, 1991), leading us to expect NPL divestiture to result in a significant reduction of bank-specific risk. More specifically, prior studies for instance have emphasized the impact of a bank's bad loans to total loans ratio upon bank-specific risk (Kwan and Eisenbeis, 1997), as weakest institutions generally exhibit higher proportions of NPL prior to failure (Berger and DeYoung, 1997; Jin et al., 2011). Assuming investor rationality, we would expect valuation effects to be related to those vendor characteristics that proxy for idiosyncratic risk. For instance, given that big transactions tremendously enhance the future prospects of these firms, we hypothesize that they should result in above-average positive shareholder wealth effects. We therefore formulate our third hypothesis as follows.

Hypothesis 3: The valuation effects observable around the announcement of NPL sales can be explained by a set of bank-specific characteristics that proxy for idiosyncratic risk as for instance a bank's ratio of NPL to total loans or the magnitude of sold NPL in percent of a bank's total assets.

While potential vendors usually have superior knowledge about the quality of their assets, the bargaining power in divestiture situations under distress is limited, while at the same time, the regulator continues to undermine the necessity of capable secondary markets (ECOFIN, 2018). With regard to real estate collateralized NPL, active resolution strategies in terms of e.g. redevelopments of underlying properties are necessary to turn from non-performing to performing assets. These endeavors encompass high amounts of risk and investors willing to bear these risks tend to be limited. Typically, investors willing to engage within these high-risk transactions are considered to be opportunistic (Rottke and Gentgen, 2008). Shilling and Wurtzebach (2012) for instance find that funds allocated to the real estate sector in 2009 (U.S. market) primarily come from value-add and opportunistic investors. Specialized institutional bidders on the buy-side are highly experienced in the valuation of NPL portfolios. Linked to the net effect of distinct attributes of real estate, a demanding skillset is needed to manage the workout of real estate collateral. Driven by different opportunity cost of capital, we would expect the opportunistic investors' buying position to be most accentuated in NPL divestiture situations that involve real estate collateral. We therefore hypothesize as follows.

Hypothesis 4: The largest buyer group of real estate collateralized NPLs are opportunistic investors, rather than other types of investors as for instance (investment) banks.

The remainder of this paper is devoted to data synthesis, formal methodology and the presentation of results.

4.3 Data and Methodology

4.3.1 Data Set

Our analysis concentrates on announcement effects of NPL divestitures in the securities market based on the event study methodology. This methodology is accredited to the seminal work of Fama et al. (1969)[1] and allows to estimate the impact of new and unexpected information on a company's market-based perception of corporate value (MacKinlay, 1997). In efficient capital markets, it is expected that security prices always correctly reflect all publicly available information (Fama, 1970). Having received broad attention in corporate finance research, event study methodology today serves as the central instrument in event-induced research (Corrado, 2011; Kothari and Warner, 2007). Corrado (2011) structurally documents the advancement of short-term event study methodology and its many applications, and Binder (1998) gives a critical review of the theoretical advancement since 1969, including hypothesis testing and the use of different benchmarks for the estimation of expected returns. The basis of every event study is a thorough event selection and cleaning process.

Initial event selection. We accumulate publicly available NPL transaction data for the period January 1st 2012 to December 31st 2018. We start to identify NPL deal announcements using Debtwire's NPL Coverage database, that actively reports information about NPL trades. Next, we apply deep learning based text recognition techniques using Tesseract to gather deal data from publicly available NPL research reports. The two main sources in the segment are industry advisors Deloitte and Cushman Wakefield. This first quest leads to a possible identification of 709 European NPL deals. As this raw data stems from multiple resources and dates may not necessarily reflect the announcement date when the new information reaches the market, we develop a comprehensive three-step cleaning process. We visualize sample size development and the sample composition with respect to each database source in Appendix Figure C.1 of the Electronic Supplementary Material.

NPL data cleaning. First, we sort for vendor, date, and project name to identify potential

---

[1]Note, however, that prior event studies in the field have been conducted by Dolley (1933); Myers and Bakay (1948); Barker (1956); Ball and Brown (1968).

duplicates. Line-by-line examining conflicted data, we ensure that the highest level of deal information remains in the sample and merge duplicates if it leads to more detailed information. In this step, 605 deals remain in the sample. Second, we run several availability checks. The name of the vendor has to be disclosed unequivocally, the date of the announcement has to be clear, the collateral type has to be known and also the country of collateral. More importantly, we match for unique identifiers in each category by hand. Where possible, we control for acquirers, detailed loan status and book value of the loans and match the information in a unified format. Having confirmed normal distribution of daily data, we first employ the 15th day of a month if only the event month of a deal is available. To ensure valid results, we later review announcement dates for all NPL deals that appear in the event study by hand. We particularly cross-check news announcements to ensure for the earliest arrival of new events in the market. Transactions in GBP-currency are converted to Euro at the historic exchange rate. NPL divestitures that were cancelled or only rumored about are exempted from the study. We group collateral types into four larger categories, namely real estate, consumer, corporate, and mixed loans. In this initial "descriptive sample", 476 NPL sales remain and are functional to characterize the European NPL market.

Banking and market data. For event study inclusion, vendors have to be a publicly listed financial institution, with liquid daily trading data during the 140 trading days preceding and 20 trading days following the event date, applying an event cutoff-date of 31st October 2018 due to the benchmark measure of normal returns discussed below. Attributing (European) subsidiary institutes to parent banks, if reasonable, we identify daily return data for 58 banks in the sample using Thomson Reuters Datastream. We retrieve daily percentage changes of the Datastream Return Index as daily stock returns in Euro, adjusted by dividends. We mark the occurrence of confounding events, i.e. NPL sales by banks within the event window of another deal by the same vendor, to control for a possible bias of our results. We check for robustness by including and excluding these follow-up events in the sample, but find that they should remain in the study as test results are not affected qualitatively. In addition to the return data, we collect a set of bank-specific variables from Thomson Financial Datastream to use both in the cross-sectional regression analysis of abnormal returns as well as in the descriptive characterization of vendors. As benchmark measure for normal returns, we obtain data for the Sharpe (1964)-Lintner (1965, 1969) model by applying the MSCI Europe as a proxy for the European market index. As additional audit of robustness, we obtain the corresponding data for the STXE 600 banks, that sector-specifically covers the 47 largest European banks, based on their market capitalization. As a proxy for the risk-free rate, we apply the EU AAA-rated government bond yield rate with a 10-year maturity. Last, we drop all vendors without liquid daily trading data (measured in zero-percent return days) during the 140 trading days preceding and 20 days following the announcement date to ensure sufficient liquidity across the sample as NPL sales may coincide with financial turbulence of the seller themselves. This final step resulted in an event study sample of 317 NPL trades with a GBV in excess of €300bn from 58 financial institutions.

In Tables 4.1 and Appendix Table C.1 of the Electronic Supplementary Material, we provide summary stats for both this reduced event study sample as well as the larger descriptive sample to account for a potential bias due to excluding financial institutions that are un-listed or have insufficient daily and liquid return data. Both panels are consistent. With regards to transaction volumes, while the smaller single-name transactions or portfolio bas-kets start with smaller GBVs of €5m, the largest transactions amount up to €26bn face value. These large block transactions oftentimes account for NPL disposal into bad-banks or similar government endowed entities. Note, GBVs do not represent actual transaction prices.

Table 4.1 reports the different collateral classes in the sample. The mapping procedure for collateral types is documented in Appendix Table C.5 of the Electronic Supplementary Material. Based on a mere GBV-valuation, app. two thirds of the collateral (66.1%) are real estate loans. The other third accounts for consumer loans (5.7%), corporate loans (4.0%), and mixed loan pools (24.2%). Regarding the latter category, these loans represent a mixture of the other three loan types in an unknown proportion. For this reason, we estimate the actual real estate proportion to be higher. Real estate and mixed loan pools together pinpoint the dominant and distinct role of real estate collateral in the European distressed loan sale market, yielding a first indication regarding our second hypothesis.

Table 4.1: Distribution of Collateral Types

This table reports summary statistics for the initial NPL sample (*n=476*) as well as our event study sample (*n=317*) on estimated actual and relative GBVs of realized transactions for each collateral type, respectively. We recalculate GBP (£) to Euro with the respective exchange rate at the date of the transaction.

Type of Collateral	Estimated GBV in €bn	Relative (%)
Panel A: Descriptive Sample		
All Assets (*n=476*)	490.06	100.0%
Real Estate (*n=300*)	324.11	66.1%
Consumer (*n=58*)	27.81	5.7%
Corporate (*n=41*)	19.78	4.0%
Mixed Loan Pool (*n=77*)	118.35	24.2%
Panel B: Event Study Sample		
All Assets (*=317*)	308.40	100.0%
Real Estate (*n=188*)	202.38	65.6%
Consumer (*n=45*)	21.36	6.9%
Corporate (*n=28*)	14.59	4.7%
Mixed Loan Pool (*n=56*)	70.07	22.7%

Appendix Table C.1 of the Electronic Supplementary Material reports an overview of the top transaction parties (both vendors and acquirers) as well as key transaction markets for both the larger descriptive market sample as well as the event study example. In regards to the country assignment of a transaction, we hypothesize some ambiguity in the data at this point, as many portfolio deals involve collateral from multiple countries, yet independent from the location of the vendor. Nevertheless, in line with industry expert and regulatory commentators, the majority of transactions in the sample stems from Italy, Spain and the UK (70.0%). For this approximation, we later include a binary dummy for Italy in the multivariate regression since Italian deals represent the largest subgroup. Considering the dominant buyer groups, the opportunistic private equity funds Cerberus, Lone Star and Blackstone account for a third of the deal volume. The largest single buyer party are securitizations or sales to consortia of multiple buyers, which we cannot assign precisely (15.9%). Thus, we explore these structures in more detail using logistic-regressions in Section 4.4.4. Considering the sell-side, the present sample appears rather homogeneous, as the five largest vendors account for much less of the market volume (30.1%) compared to the acquirer group (51.3%). In line with anticipated media coverage, the largest single vendors are Banca Monte dei Paschi di Siena (6.8%), UKAR (i.e. UK Asset Resolution; 6.3%), Banco Santander (6.1%), and NAMA (Ireland Asset resolution vehicle; 5,7%). In addition, in Appendix Table C.2 of the Electronic Supplementary Material, we report the yearly distribution of the transactions for both samples and also account for a time-fixed effect in the robustness checks of the event study.

Table 4.2: Key Financial Characteristics of Vendors in the Event Study Sample

This table presents the key financial characteristics for the 58 vendor banks in the event study sample ($n=317$). Balance sheet items reflect year-end results. Items are reported in €bn for convenience.

	Overall Sample ($n=317$)	Real Estate Subsample ($n=188$)
Panel A: Total Assets in €bn		
Mean	673.00	620.00
Standard Deviation	538.00	451.00
Min.	1.28	1.28
Max.	2,377.43	2,377.43
Panel B: NPL in €bn		
Mean	21.50	18.50
Standard Deviation	20.02	18.50
Min.	0.13	0.59
Max.	84.40	79.80
Panel C: NPL % Total Loans		
Mean	9.79	9.26
Standard Deviation	7.90	6.55
Min.	0.30	0.30
Max.	63.13	31.77
Panel D: NPL % Equity		
Mean	97.18	93.06
Standard Deviation	82.26	75.04
Min.	3.13	3.13
Max.	541.51	333.13
Panel E: ROA 5-Year Average in %		
Mean	0.61	0.64
Standard Deviation	0.55	0.54
Min.	-2.63	-1.06
Max.	7.17	7.17

Table 4.2 reports the key financial characteristics for the vendors of the smaller event study sample ($n=317$), where we are able to retrieve the corresponding financial data from the Datastream database. Again, the event study sample serves as fair proxy of the larger descriptive sample of the current NPL market. The data shows the expected concentration

of key ratios within our sample of firms divesting loans under distress.

4.3.2 Methodology

We measure short-term valuation effects of banks' NPL divestiture announcements by applying common event study methodology. Thus, we first require a benchmark measure of
normal returns (Brown and Warner, 1980; MacKinlay, 1997), as abnormal returns are defined
as actual ex-post returns over the event window, exceeding returns that would have been
expected without the event taking place (MacKinlay, 1997). As this paper entirely deals
with equities from the financial industry, note that the performance of more sophisticated
multi-factor models, such as the Fama and French (1993) three-factor model is disputed for
explaining the cross-section of banking stocks (see Viale et al. (2009)). Thus, we first employ the one factor Sharpe (1964)-Lintner (1965, 1969) capital asset pricing model (CAPM),
based on the MSCI Europe, followed by an analysis of robustness using deviations from market adjusted returns that account for sector-specific bank returns in the European financial
industry, namely the STXE 600 banks. We measure expected normal returns using CAPM,
calculating a stock's daily return as follows:

$$E\left(R_{it}\middle|\, X_t\right) = rf_t + \beta_i MKTRF_t + \alpha_{it} \tag{1}$$

where $E\left(R_{it}\middle|\, X_t\right)$ indicates the expected daily normal return for each bank i at time t, de-
pendent upon the conditioning information X_t of our chosen asset pricing model (MacKinlay,
1997). Variable rf_t denotes the risk-free rate which we proxy by the EU AAA-rated government bond yield rate (10-year maturity). $MKTRF_t$ is the excess return on the European
equity market, i.e. the return on the MSCI Europe minus the risk-free rate, and α_{it} indicates
security-specific error terms. We apply both a 140 and an extended 273 trading day estimation window to ensure robustness of the results. The event period itself is not included in
the estimation period "to prevent the event from influencing the normal performance model
parameter estimates" (MacKinlay, 1997, p. 15). Respective betas are then used to predict
normal stock returns over the event window. Considering the short-term horizon of the estimation (cf. Barber Lyon, 1996), we decide to estimate abnormal returns for each financial

institution i, by calculating respective daily abnormal returns (AR) in comparison to the one factor-model:

$$AR_{it} = R_{it} - E\left(R_{it}\mid X_t\right) \tag{2}$$

ARs are calculated over a whole 41-day event window from T_1 to T_2, comprised of 20 pre-event days ($t=-20$), one event day, and 20 post-event days ($t=+20$). We define the event t_0 to be the earliest announcement of NPL divestiture during the timespan January 1st 2012 to October 31st 2018. Next, we aggregate abnormal returns of stock returns for all events respectively (CAR):

$$CAR_{iT_1,T_2} = \sum_{t=T_1}^{T_2} AR_{it} \tag{3}$$

where CAR_i is the cumulative abnormal return for a financial institution i and T_1, T_2 indicates the event window. Last, we report the cumulative average abnormal returns $CAAR_{T_1,T_2}$ over the chosen event window throughout all NPL divestiture announcements for stocks:

$$CAAR_{T_1,T_2} = \frac{1}{N}\sum_{i=1}^{N}\sum_{i=T_1}^{T_2} AR_{it} \tag{4}$$

We employ the parametric test statistics of Boehmer et al. (1991) and the non-parametric test statistics of Corrado and Corrado and Zivney (1992) to test for the statistical significance of ARs and CARs aggregated over all financial institutions in the sample. Further, we control for changes between median and mean CAARs. We apply the same methodology on a number of subsamples across different collateral classes and for the robustness checks.

Following preceding analyses, we perform multivariate regression analyses to identify key value drivers of abnormal returns following NPL divestiture announcements, using a series of bank-specific deal characteristics. In this paper, we employ cross-sectional analyses of the form:

$$CAR_{iT_1, T_2} = \gamma_0 + \gamma_1 npl\_tl_i + \gamma_2 roa\_5_i + \gamma_3 ceq\_ta_i + \gamma_4 loanloss\_rll_i + \gamma_5 capad_i + \quad (5)$$

$$\gamma_6 gbvnpl\_ta_i + \gamma_7 italy\_dummy_i + \gamma_8 re\_dummy_i + \epsilon_i$$

where we apply observed CARs for the [-5; +5] event window as dependent variable. npl_tl_i is defined as a bank's NPL to total loans ratio, roa_5_i is the bank's five-year average return on assets (ROA), ceq_ta_i the firm-specific common equity to total assets ratio, $loanloss\_rll_i$ indicates a bank's actual loan losses in percent of reserves for loan losses, $capad_i$ reports the respective Tier 1 capital adequacy ratio, and $gbvnpl\_ta_i$ the ratio of sold NPL's gross book value (GBV) to the respective bank's total assets. Next, due to the high number of NPL deals announced in Italy, we include a binary Italy dummy. Finally, we include a dummy variable indicating whether (1) or not (0) respective NPL deals are collateralized by real estate. Standard errors are clustered on vendor-level. All data for bank-specific characteristics is obtained via Thomson Reuters Datastream/Worldscope. Detailed variable explanations and calculations are presented in Appendix Table C.3 of the Electronic Supplementary Material.

Last, we perform logistic regressions to analyze the relationship between distinct types of investors and underlying NPL collaterals. For this purpose, we classify investors into five categories as follows: specialized (small) investors ($buyer\_type$ 1), opportunity funds ($buyer\_type$ 2), consortia of multiple buyers / securitization ($buyer\_type$ 3), (investment-) banks ($buyer\_type$ 4), and undisclosed investors ($buyer\_type$ 5). We start by using the real estate dummy of the overall event study sample ($n=317$) as dependent variable, indicating whether the respective NPL is collateralized by real estate. As predictors, we choose the above-mentioned set of firm characteristics and buyer types, respectively and thus run logistic regressions as follows:

$$P(re\_dummy = 1|X) = G(\gamma_0 + \gamma_1 npl\_tl_i + \gamma_2 roa\_5_i + \gamma_3 ceq\_ta_i + \quad (6)$$

$$\gamma_4 loanloss\_rll_i + \gamma_5 capad_i + \gamma_6 gbvnpl\_ta_i + \gamma_7 italy\_dummy_i +$$

$$\gamma_8 buyer\_type_i)$$

where $P\left(re\_dummy = 1 \mid X\right)$ indicates the probability of being a real estate collateralized NPL transaction conditional upon our chosen set of bank-specific characteristics. G is a specific function taking values between 0 and 1, when applying logistic regression. Additionally, as a robustness check, we run logistic regressions using each buyer type as dependent variable, respectively. When running corresponding logistic regressions, the maximum likelihood estimation method is used.

4.4   Empirical Results

4.4.1   Abnormal Returns Following NPL Divestiture Announcements

We begin the analysis by concentrating on the short-term valuation effect following the announcement of NPL divestitures at European banks. For each announcement, we test our first hypothesis that the announcing banks experience significant positive valuation, as measured by the cumulative abnormal returns of the vendor.

In Table 4.3, we report our baseline event study results around the announcement dates for the 58 banks in the sample. Panel A documents our first model, the Sharpe (1964)-Lintner (1965, 1969) one factor asset pricing model, based on the MSCI Europe. Mean CAR amounts to 1.71%, significant at the 1%-level (z-score: 3.76) for the [-5; +5] event window. In Panel B, we present a market estimation robustness, based on the STXE 600 bank index, representing the movement of the 47 largest European banks. Mean CAR declines by 29 bps to 1.42% in Panel B, again significant at the 1%-level (z-score: 3.90).

CAARs are tested for statistical significance using both the parametric test by (Boehmer et al., 1991) and the non-parametric test procedure, introduced by (Corrado and Zivney, 1992), that test the hypothesis that CAARs equal zero. Our findings are robust across both statistics and we also monitor for sign changes between mean and median CARs, again affirming the result during the significant event window [-5; +5]. We estimate CAARs over multiple event windows, with the maximum event window being [-20; +20] and an estimation window of [-140; -21].

Table 4.3: Abnormal Stock Returns Following NPL Divestiture Announcements

This table shows the stock market reaction following 317 NPL divestiture announcements at 58 banks. *, **, *** indicate statistical significance at the 10%, 5%, and 1% level, respectively.

Event Window Days (t)	Panel A: MSCI Europe ($n=317$)				Panel B: STXE 600 Banks ($n=317$)			
	CAAR (%)	Median CAR (%)	BMP test	CZ test	CAAR (%)	Median CAR (%)	BMP test	CZ test
$[-20; +20]$	0.76	0.67	0.46	-0.39	0.47	0.38	1.10	0.10
$[-10; +10]$	0.00	-0.24	-0.25	-0.81	0.14	-0.38	0.48	-0.24
$[-5; +5]$	1.71	0.76	3.76***	2.00**	1.42	1.06	3.90***	2.25**
$[-1; +1]$	0.52	0.06	2.35**	1.05	0.50	0.07	2.48**	1.40
$[0; +0]$	0.33	0.08	1.92*	1.15	0.30	0.10	2.07**	1.32
$[0; +1]$	0.44	0.01	2.05*	1.20	0.44	0.15	2.29**	1.49
$[0; +5]$	0.98	0.17	2.52**	1.99**	0.81	0.39	3.36***	2.31**
$[0; +20]$	-0.14	-0.49	-0.53	-0.65	-0.06	-0.52	0.27	-0.13

As additional audit of coherence, we have checked the robustness with an extended estimation window of [-273; -21], i.e. one full trading year, but the results are not affected quantitatively. Furthermore, we mark the occurrence of confounding events, i.e. NPL sales by banks within the event window of another deal by the same vendor, to control for a possible bias of our results. We check for robustness by including and excluding these follow-up events in the sample, but find that they should remain in the study as test results are not affected qualitatively. Furthermore, we do not detect a time-fixed effect, analyzing deals for each year separately.

We interpret our results as a clear indication affirming the first hypothesis, that announcements of NPL divestiture caused positive valuation effects, as abnormal returns are defined as actual ex-post returns over the event window, exceeding returns that would have been expected without the event taking place (MacKinlay, 1997). This finding underpins earlier results by Geiger et al. (2007) on a much broader basis and - in contrast to the findings of Dahiya et al. (2003) - indicates that NPL divestiture activity generated shareholder wealth in the short-term. We assert this early finding to the fact that failing banks generally report significant proportions of NPL prior to failure or distress (Berger and DeYoung, 1997; Jin et al., 2011), and thus interpret the sale of non-performing assets as a signaling about the vendor's willingness to ensure smooth functioning after negative shocks (Granja et al., 2017).

Banks currently operate under increasing regulatory and supervisory pressure to dispose of NPL (ECB, 2018a,b). In this regard, the signaling about smooth functioning after negative shocks is extended by showing security holders the willingness to comply to regulatory pressure.

On the contrary, considering longer event windows around the announcement date, such as [-20; +20], the positive valuation effect appears to vanish over time. We interpret this finding as a first indicator that information related to NPL sale announcements tends to be priced rather quickly within the equity market and in favor of the idea of a short-term signaling effect. This potentially corroborates an information-efficient pricing of assets under distress and leads to potential negative returns in the longer term. Thus far, our findings therefore do not raise doubts about the ability of market participants to generate information efficient valuations of NPLs that are primarily collateralized by real estate (cash flows). Regarding a deeper interpretation of this result, in particular regarding changes of leverage and relative size of sold NPL, more analyses during sections 4.4.2 and 4.4.3 appear necessary.

4.4.2   Real Estate Driven Abnormal Returns

An important aspect to regulators and banks' decision-makers alike is whether the valuation effect is driven by specific types of collateral, considering the liquidated assets of banks' balance sheets. Thus, we split the overall event study sample into four smaller buckets, for each type of underlying collateral accordingly. We generally employ the same methodology and test statistics as for the overall analysis in Section 4.4.1.

The value of real estate NPL portfolios is largely determined by (expected) rental income and (potential) property sale proceeds in the real estate market. Figure 4.1 compares CAARs resulting from NPL sale announcements for each day of the significant [-5; +5] event window of the overall sample ($n=317$) as well as a subsample exhibiting NPL sales with real estate collateral ($n=188$). This evaluation is based on the one-factor pricing model applying the MSCI Europe as the corresponding market return (i.e. Panel A in Table 3). Employing the market return estimation based on the bank index as robustness did yield the same result, and for reasons of brevity is thus not shown in the paper (i.e. Panel B in Table 3).

Figure 4.1: Cumulative Average Abnormal Returns Following
NPL Divestiture Announcements

This figure shows the cumulative average abnormal return performance of the sample for real estate collateral ($n=188$) and the overall NPL sample ($n=317$) during 2012-2018. The Sharpe (1964)-Lintner (1965, 1969) capital asset pricing model is used by applying the MSCI Europe for the computation of CAARs.

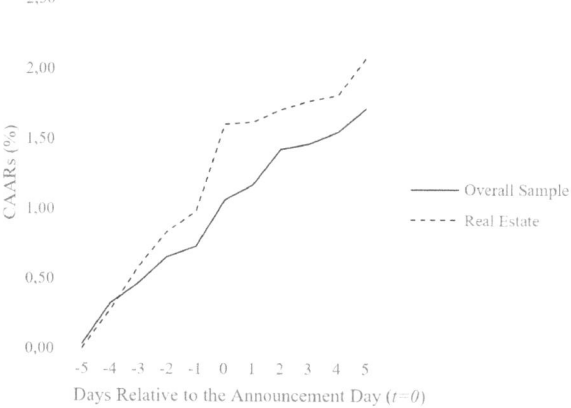

Figure 4.1 highlights that the positive valuation effect is more severe for NPL sales collateralized by real estate as compared to the overall sample. The excess return of 37 bps of the real estate sample during the event window [-5; +5] as compared to the overall sample is highly significant, yielding evidence in favor of our second hypothesis.

Along this line of interpretation, Table 4.4 displays a more detailed analysis of each collateral class separately. Regarding the real estate sample, results are significant at the 1% level (z-score:3.86). In addition to our main event window [-5; +5], CAARs for the [-1; +1] event window increases from 0.52% to 0.79% and from 0.33% to 0.62% for the [0; +0] event window. Statistical significance of the windows [-1; +1] and [0; +0] increases in the real estate sample accordingly. At the same time, the lack of significance for the non-real estate subsamples should be interpreted with caution. The power of the test statistics decreases with the smaller sample sizes of consumer loans ($n=45$), corporate loans ($n=28$), and mixed loans ($n=56$), increasing the probability of an error of type II about the null hypothesis H_0. We acknowledge from prior descriptive statistics in Table 4.1 that the distribution of deals in the event study sample is indeed representative for the secondary NPL market in Europe to the best of our knowledge.

Table 4.4: Abnormal Stock Returns Per Collateral Type

This table shows the stock market reaction following 317 NPL divestiture announcements at 58 banks for each collateral class separately. *, **, *** indicate statistical significance at the 10%, 5%, and 1% level, respectively.

Event Window Days (t)	CAAR (%)	Median CAR (%)	BMP test (z-score)	CZ test (z-score)
Real Estate Loans (n=188)				
$[-10; +10]$	0.27	-0.10	0.41	-0.61
$[-5; +5]$	2.08	0.98	3.86***	2.40**
$[-1; +1]$	0.79	0.40	2.68***	1.53
$[0; +0]$	0.62	0.25	3.30***	2.43**
Consumer Loans (n=45)				
$[-10; +10]$	1.05	0.41	0.22	0.65
$[-5; +5]$	2.07	0.31	0.86	0.60
$[-1; +1]$	-0.02	-0.74	0.25	-0.09
$[0; +0]$	-0.27	-0.27	-0.54	-0.63
Corporate Loans (n=28)				
$[-10; +10]$	0.87	-0.98	-0.26	-0.49
$[-5; +5]$	1.43	-0.19	-0.13	-0.13
$[-1; +1]$	-0.18	-0.10	-0.92	-0.58
$[0; +0]$	-0.23	-0.01	-1.17	-0.93
Mixed Loan Pool (n=56)				
$[-10; +10]$	-2.16	-1.00	-1.23	-1.35
$[-5; +5]$	0.33	0.98	1.40	0.24
$[-1; +1]$	0.40	-0.09	0.93	0.38
$[0; +0]$	0.13	-0.19	0.11	-0.25

Results from Figure 4.1 and Table 4.4 together pinpoint that capital markets evaluate the sales of real estate NPL portfolios to be relatively more attractive as compared to other kinds of NPL portfolios in the short-term. We interpret this observation as the net effect of distinct real estate attributes. Its tangibility gives both vendor and the acquirer the opportunity to estimate its intrinsic value and facilitates the evaluation compared to the appraisal of corporate or unsecured consumer debt. The result affirms our second hypothesis and adds to a trending research topic, namely accounting for real estate separately in NPL research

(Adelino et al., 2016; Beck et al., 2015; Ghosh, 2015). To verify a more specific possible interpretation of this finding, we perform a cross-sectional analysis of abnormal returns in the next subsection.

4.4.3 Cross-Sectional Analyses of Abnormal Returns

We continue the analysis by testing our third hypothesis, implying that CARs can be explained by a set of accounting variables that proxy for idiosyncratic risk, in a quest to understand the key value drivers of abnormal returns following NPL sale announcements. To obtain first insights on how bank-specific vendor characteristics relate to abnormal returns, we sort corresponding CARs into deciles, applying results obtained from the [-5; +5] event window due to its highest statistical significance (from lowest to highest CARs; P1 to P10). For each CAR decile, we report cross-sectional averages of cumulative abnormal returns as well as cross-sectional averages of the following bank-specific variables: NPL to total loans ratio (npl_tl), NPL to equity ratio (npl_eq), five-year average return on assets (roa_5y), common equity to total assets ratio (ceq_ta), actual loan losses in percent of reserves for loan losses ($loanloss\_rll$), Tier 1 capital adequacy ratio ($capad$), ratio of sold NPL's GBV to bank's total assets ($gbvnpl\_ta$) and the $italy\_dummy$. Table 4.5 summarizes corresponding results. Panel A reports findings for our overall sample ($n=317$). Panel B presents insights obtained from the real estate subsample ($n=188$).

As presented in Table 4.5, average cumulative abnormal returns range from lowest -8.42% to highest 16.58% within Panel A. Notably, deals that are conducted by banks exhibiting highest NPL to total loans ratios (npl_tl) as well as highest NPL to equity ratios (npl_eq), and highest ratios of sold NPL's GBV to bank's total assets ($gbvnpl\_ta$) are the ones yielding highest abnormal returns (P10). We interpret this result as a first indication of a size effect, driven by the relative size of the liquidation of risky assets.

Table 4.5: Decile Sorting of Cumulative Abnormal Returns

This table summarizes average cumulative abnormal returns and average firm-specific characteristics of portfolios sorted on past cumulative abnormal returns for the [-5; +5] event window using the MSCI Europe as respective benchmark. Panel A reports findings for our overall sample ($n=317$). Panel B summarizes insights obtained from the real estate subsample ($n=188$). To construct portfolios, we sort cumulative abnormal returns into deciles. Within each decile portfolio, we then report cross-sectional averages of cumulative abnormal returns for the [-5; +5] event window as well as cross-sectional averages of the following bank-specific variables: NPL to total loans ratio (npl_tl), NPL to equity ratio (npl_eq), five-year average return on assets (roa_5y), common equity to total assets ratio (ceq_ta), actual loan losses in percent of reserves for loan losses ($loanloss\_rll$), Tier 1 capital adequacy ratio ($capad$), ratio of sold NPL's GBV to bank's total assets ($gbvnpl\_ta$) and the *italy_dummy*. Detailed variable explanations and calculations are presented in Appendix Table C.3 of the Electronic Supplementary Material.

	P1	P2	P3	P4	P5	P6	P7	P8	P9	P10
Panel A: Total Sample ($n=317$)										
CAR [-5; +5]	-8.42	-3.94	-1.98	-0.54	0.35	1.36	2.68	4.39	7.16	16.58
npl_tl	9.93	8.81	10.15	7.83	10.83	6.66	8.02	9.18	14.79	12.27
npl_eq	100.04	88.40	100.22	77.96	97.72	67.41	75.92	87.38	151.61	128.94
roa_5y	0.51	0.65	0.56	0.80	0.47	0.68	0.60	0.58	0.47	0.76
ceq_ta	6.01	6.56	6.38	7.53	6.54	6.18	6.53	6.35	7.55	6.96
$loanloss\_rll$	20.74	23.49	22.78	28.33	19.41	26.46	21.46	21.53	22.38	21.47
$capad$	12.97	13.77	14.07	13.60	13.74	13.49	13.31	13.53	13.53	13.40
$gbvnpl\_ta$	0.50	0.81	0.79	0.76	0.57	0.74	0.57	1.51	1.34	1.90
italy_dummy	0.30	0.43	0.15	0.17	0.22	0.29	0.33	0.32	0.32	0.40
Panel B: Real Estate Subsample ($n=188$)										
CAR [-5; +5]	-8.53	-3.18	-1.46	-0.45	0.50	1.45	3.09	4.80	7.48	14.01
npl_tl	8.59	8.26	6.74	8.27	9.25	3.71	9.97	8.89	14.65	11.29
npl_eq	86.12	83.61	64.39	80.11	92.26	33.56	100.67	81.20	158.74	115.25
roa_5y	0.56	0.61	0.60	1.17	0.58	0.71	0.73	0.53	0.61	0.61
ceq_ta	5.88	5.97	6.48	9.92	6.36	5.79	6.07	6.72	6.54	6.07
$loanloss\_rll$	28.11	35.65	44.82	27.02	23.75	32.73	21.69	35.45	20.80	29.86
$capad$	12.91	14.30	14.64	14.09	13.38	13.54	13.01	14.41	13.50	13.59
$gbvnpl\_ta$	0.28	0.35	0.95	0.83	0.66	0.37	0.81	1.22	0.40	3.91
italy_dummy	0.33	0.08	0.08	0.00	0.17	0.08	0.17	0.17	0.27	0.27

Concerning the real estate subsample, average cumulative abnormal returns range from lowest -8.53% to highest 14.01%. Again, highest returns are obtained for banks exhibiting highest NPL to total loans ratios (npl_tl) as well as highest NPL to equity ratios (npl_eq), and highest ratios of sold NPL's GBV to bank's total assets ($gbvnpl\_ta$). Within both panels, lowest (P1) and highest (P10) returns seem to be driven by Italian NPL deals that represent the largest country subgroup in the sample.

To analyze the relationship between bank-specific characteristics and observed abnormal returns in more detail, we next perform cross-sectional regression analyses using observed CARs for our overall sample ($n=317$) as dependent variable. As explanatory variables, we apply the above-listed set of firm-specific characteristics with the exception of NPL to equity ratios (npl_eq) to avoid potential multicollinearity issues. Additionally, we add a real estate dummy within the regression analysis, indicating whether respective NPLs are collateralized by real estate. Table 4.6 summarizes cross-sectional regression results using CARs for the following event windows: [-5; +5] in Panel A, [-10; +10] in Panel B as well as [-20; +20] in Panel C. Within each panel, the left column reports results obtained from applying the MSCI Europe. The right column illustrates findings once applying the STXE 600 bank index.

As shown in Table 4.6, company characteristics exhibiting statistical significance in explaining CARs within the [-5; +5] event window are a firm's NPL to total loans ratio (npl_tl) (5% significance level) as well as the ratio of sold NPL's GBV to banks' total assets ($gbvnpl\_ta$) (1% significance level). Statistical significances of these variables even increase once applying the STXE 600 bank index instead of the MSCI Europe. Whereas there exists a positive economic link between a firm's NPL to total loans ratio and its respective abnormal returns, firms exhibiting higher common equity to total assets ratios (ceq_ta) tend to show a more negative performance. Additionally, the five-year average return on assets (roa_5y) as well as actual loan losses in percent of reserves for loan losses ($loanloss\_rll$) turn statistically significant at the 5% level once applying the STXE 600 bank index rather than the MSCI Europe. These results underline various facets of a size effect. Relatively large NPL portfolio sales unburden the restructuring teams in vendor banks significantly more than smaller sales. But a portfolio sale of a given size is more helpful for a bank with a lower level of common equity because these institutions become more stable after the transaction. More ECB pressure on the weakest financial institutions to clean balance sheets from distressed assets will result in short-term above-average revaluation of bank equity.

Table 4.6: Cross-Sectional Sell-Side Regression Results

This table reports OLS regression results for the overall event study sample of 317 events. As dependent variable we apply cumulative abnormal returns for the following event windows: [-5; +5] in Panel A; [-10; +10] in Panel B; [-20; +20] in Panel C. We apply the following bank-specific explanatory variables: NPL to total loans ratio (npl_tl), five-year average return on assets (roa_5y), common equity to total assets ratio (ceq_ta), actual loan losses in percent of reserves for loan losses ($loanloss\_rll$), Tier 1 capital adequacy ratio ($capad$), ratio of sold NPL's GBV to bank's total assets ($gbvnpl\_ta$) as well as an Italy dummy ($italy\_dummy$) and a real estate dummy (re_dummy). Detailed variable explanations and calculations are presented in Appendix Table C.3 of the Electronic Supplementary Material. Standard errors are clustered on vendor-level. CAPM refers to the Sharpe (1964)-Lintner (1965, 1969) pricing model, based on the MSCI Europe; STXE 600 refers to our robustness check for the cross-section of banking stocks. *, **, *** indicate statistical significance at the 10%, 5%, and 1% level, respectively.

	Panel A		Panel B		Panel C	
	Dependent Variable CAR [-5; +5]		Dependent Variable CAR [-10; +10]		Dependent Variable CAR [-20; +20]	
	MSCI Europe	STXE 600	MSCI Europe	STXE 600	MSCI Europe	STXE 600
npl_tl	0.24**	0.22***	0.11	0.14	0.18	0.06
	(2.14)	(2.76)	(1.19)	(1.39)	(0.98)	(0.43)
roa_5y	1.75	1.99**	-0.82	0.41	-0.72	-1.68
	(1.11)	(2.17)	(-0.46)	(0.28)	(-0.19)	(-0.65)
ceq_ta	-0.25	-0.33**	0.02	-0.29	-0.08	0.01
	(-0.79)	(-2.23)	(0.06)	(-1.29)	(-0.11)	(0.02)
$loanloss\_rll$	0.01	0.03**	0.01	0.05***	0.00	0.02
	(0.42)	(2.04)	(0.53)	(3.05)	(-0.01)	(1.27)
$capad$	-0.10	-0.13	0.48	0.09	1.04	0.10
	(0.27)	(-0.66)	(1.22)	(0.34)	(1.60)	(0.21)
$gbvnpl\_ta$	0.21***	0.32***	0.61***	0.57***	0.12	0.26
	(3.00)	(3.99)	(4.42)	(4.58)	(0.64)	(1.24)
$italy\_dummy$	0.44	-0.01	-0.21	0.38	-4.63***	-1.98
	(0.44)	(-0.01)	(-0.18)	(0.36)	(-2.67)	(-1.47)
re_dummy	0.26	0.02	1.07	-0.68	-2.60	0.17
	(0.31)	(0.02)	(0.88)	(-0.71)	(-1.29)	(0.15)
$CONSTANT$	0.57	1.14	-9.23	-2.15	-12.74	-0.80
	(0.14)	(0.41)	(-1.58)	(-0.49)	(-1.20)	(-0.11)
R^2	0.070	0.087	0.068	0.083	0.071	0.036
$F-value$	5.95	4.69	6.57	7.86	4.74	1.88

For the [-10; +10] event window, the explanatory power of a firm's NPL to total loans ratio (*npl_tl*) disappears in both columns. Conversely, statistical significance of the variable *gbvnpl_ta* even increases within both columns of Panel B. Once taking into account the [-20; +20] event window, the explanatory power of the variables *npl_tl*, *roa_5y*, *ceq_ta*, *loanloss_rll* and *gbvnpl_ta* disappears entirely. This finding confirms baseline event study results reported in Section 4.4.1. Information related to NPL sale announcements tend to be priced quickly within the equity market. Thus, the explanatory power of bank-specific characteristics concerning abnormal returns following NPL sale announcements vanishes over time once taking into consideration longer event windows. We interpret these findings as a confirmation of our third hypothesis, stating that valuation effects observable around the announcement of NPL sales can be explained by a set of bank-specific characteristics that proxy for idiosyncratic risk, as for instance the bank's ratio of NPL to total loans, its common equity in percent of total assets, and the GBV of sold NPL in percent of a bank's total assets.

Our main results imply that announcements of NPL divestiture result in positive valuation effects of European vendor banks. The announcement effect is strongest for real estate NPL portfolios as compared to other kinds of NPLs. We have ensured validity of these findings in multiple ways, including the application of extended estimation windows as well as the exclusion of confounding events.

To test for the robustness of the explanatory power of reported bank characteristics, we additionally conduct four robustness checks, which are provided in Appendix C of the Electronic Supplementary Material. Specifically, we rely on several fixed-effects regressions, leaving either collateral type, buyer type, vendor bank, or NPL-size constant. When running fixed-effects regressions, we apply the least squares dummy variable model (LSDV). In line with equation (5), we use observed CARs for the [-5; +5], [-10; +10] as well as the [-20; +20] event window as dependent variables and our previously specified set of bank characteristics as corresponding independent variables.

The main result of our additional robustness checks is that the size-effect (*gbvnpl_ta*) remains statistically significant in explaining abnormal returns within all of the above-listed regression specifications (ranging between the 1% and 5% significance level). In line with reported findings in Section 4.4.3, our robustness tests confirm that the explanatory power of this size effect vanishes over time. In addition, we find the NPL to total loans ratio (npl_tl) to maintain its statistical significance within three out of four fixed-effects model specifications (ranging between the 5% and 10% significance level). Similar to the size-effect, the explanatory power of the NPL to total loans ratio (npl_tl) disappears over time. The findings thus underline that information related to NPL divestitures seem to be priced quickly within European equity markets. Also, in line with reported findings in the text, we document supporting evidence that over longer periods (i.e. over the [-20; +20] event window), Italian banks seem to do particularly poorly in comparison to the overall European market. However, the statistical relevance of banks' common equity in percent of total assets (ceq_ta) cannot be confirmed in any of the four fixed-effects model specifications.

Overall, the findings of additionally conducted robustness checks still support our third hypothesis, implying that valuation effects observable around the announcement of NPL sales can be explained by a set of bank-specific characteristics that proxy for idiosyncratic risk. Most significantly, we are able to validate that positive stock market reactions are driven by a size effect.

4.4.4   Cross-Sectional Buy-Side Analyses

We proceed by investigating the relationship between different types of investors and previously categorized NPL collaterals. While potential vendors usually have superior knowledge about the quality of their assets, the bargaining power in divestiture situations under distress is limited. In our fourth hypothesis, we argue that to a vast majority, real estate collateralized NPL should be acquired by opportunistic investors. We expect specialized institutional bidders on the buy-side to be highly experienced in the valuation of complex real estate NPL portfolios. We therefore perform logistic regressions, using the real estate dummy of our overall sample ($n=317$) as the dependent variable and our chosen set of bank characteristics as well as corresponding buyer types as explanatory variables.

Table 4.7 summarizes results obtained from our first-step logistic regression analysis (Panel A) and corresponding margins at means for each indicator variable (Panel B).

As shown in Table 4.7, the probability of being a real estate collateralized NPL transaction is highest when sellers exhibit high five-year average ROAs (roa_5y) while simultaneously having high actual loan losses in percent of reserves for loan losses ($loanloss\_rll$). Conversely, the probability of being a real estate collateralized transaction decreases for Italian deals. On an aggregate basis, the predicted probability of being a real estate collateralized NPL transaction is highest (0.84) for buyer type 2 (opportunity funds) and lowest for undisclosed buyers (0.19) as well as consortia of multiple buyers (0.41). Our findings imply that opportunity funds in particular tend to acquire NPL collateralized by real estate, therefore confirming our fourth and final hypothesis. We relate this finding to the specific knowledge and experience needed to cope with real estate as an asset class as well as the high potential of value creation and the risk associated within these kind of transactions.

As a robustness check, we next run logistic regressions using each buyer type as dependent variable separately. Table 4.8 summarizes respective regression results.

As shown in Table 4.8, the real estate dummy is positive and statistically significant only for buyer type 2 (opportunity funds), however, negatively significant for buyer types 3 (consortia of multiple buyers) and 5 (undisclosed investors). This finding suggests that real estate collateralized NPLs tend to be acquired by opportunistic investors while simultaneously being avoided by consortia of multiple buyers and undisclosed investors. These results overall confirm our fourth hypothesis, implying that real estate collateralized NPLs mainly tend to be acquired by opportunity funds.[2]

---

[2]Further information can be found in Appendix Table C.1 of the Electronic Supplementary Material that reports the opportunistic investors Cerberus, Lone Star and Blackstone to be active buying parties, accounting for a large oligopoly share in the secondary market that the regulator currently aims to strengthen (ECOFIN, 2018).

Table 4.7: Real Estate Logistic Regression Results

This table reports logistic regression results (Panel A) and margins at means (Panel B) for corresponding indicator variables. RE_dummy is the dependent (dummy) variable and equals 1 if the NPL is collateralized by real estate, 0 otherwise. Following prior analyses, we apply the following bank-specific characteristics as explanatory variables: NPL to total loans ratio (npl_tl), five-year average return on assets (roa_5y), common equity to total assets ratio (ceq_ta), actual loan losses in percent of reserves for loan losses ($loanloss\_rll$), Tier 1 capital adequacy ratio ($capad$), ratio of sold NPL's GBV to bank's total assets ($gbvnpl\_ta$) as well as an Italy dummy ($italy\_dummy$) and corresponding buyer types ($buyer\_type$). Detailed variable explanations and calculations are presented in Appendix Table C.3 of the Electronic Supplementary Material. Standard errors are clustered on vendor-level and indicated in parentheses. *, **, *** indicate statistical significance at the 10%, 5%, and 1% level, respectively.

	Panel A Regression Results		Panel B Margins at Means
npl_tl	0.053		
	(0.03)		
roa_5y	0.944*		
	(0.53)		
ceq_ta	-0.146		
	(0.11)		
$loanloss\_rll$	0.020**		
	(0.01)		
$capad$	-0.004		
	(0.08)		
$gbvnpl\_ta$	0.035		
	(0.06)		
$italy\_dummy$	-1.400**		$italy\_dummy$
	(0.33)	0	0.730***
			(0.047)
		1	0.400***
			(0.063)
$buyer\_type$			$buyer\_type$
2	1.252***	2	0.841***
	(0.46)		(0.051)
3	-0.767*	3	0.412***
	(0.42)		(0.081)
4	-0.040	4	0.592***
	(0.38)		(0.076)
5	-1.897***	5	0.185*
	(0.73)		(0.107)
$CONSTANT$	0.279		
	(1.13)		
$Peusdo\ R^2$	0.2069		

Table 4.8: Buyer Types Logistic Regression Results

This table reports buyer types logistic regression results. As dependent variable, we apply each buyer type, respectively, using a dummy variable which equals 1 if the NPL is acquired by a specific type, 0 otherwise. Buyer type 1 (*buyer_type* 1) represents specialized (small) investors, buyer type 2 (*buyer_type* 2) opportunity funds, buyer type 3 (*buyer_type* 3) consortia of multiple buyers / securitization, buyer type 4 (*buyer_type* 4) (investment-) banks as well as buyer type 5 (*buyer_type* 5) undisclosed investors. Again, we apply the following bank-specific characteristics as explanatory variables: NPL to total loans ratio (*npl_tl*), five-year average return on assets (*roa_5y*), common equity to total assets ratio (*ceq_ta*), actual loan losses in percent of reserves for loan losses (*loanloss_rll*), Tier 1 capital adequacy ratio (*capad*), ratio of sold NPL's GBV to bank's total assets (*gbvnpl_ta*) as well as an Italy dummy (*italy_dummy*). Additionally, we include a real estate dummy, signalling whether respective NPL deals are collateralized by real estate. Detailed variable explanations and calculations are presented in Appendix Table C.3 of the Electronic Supplementary Material. Standard errors are clustered on vendor-level and indicated in parentheses. *, **, *** indicate statistical significance at the 10%, 5%, and 1% level, respectively.

| | Panel A | Panel B | Panel C | Panel D | Panel E |
	buyer_type 1	*buyer_type* 2	*buyer_type* 3	*buyer_type* 4	*buyer_type* 5
npl_tl	0.024	-0.011	0.023	-0.053*	0.012
	(0.025)	(0.030)	(0.045)	(0.027)	(0.037)
roa_5y	-0.233	-0.116	0.349	-0.185	0.371
	(0.366)	(0.398)	(0.787)	(0.381)	(0.683)
ceq_ta	-0.031	0.048	-0.207	0.041	0.044
	(0.073)	(0.073)	(0.141)	(0.084)	(0.144)
loanloss_rll	-0.0123*	0.007	0.013*	-0.005	-0.003
	(0.007)	(0.007)	(0.007)	(0.008)	(0.013)
capad	0.023	0.017	-0.020	-0.053	-0.111
	(0.075)	(0.093)	(0.146)	(0.083)	(0.141)
gbvnpl_ta	0.053	-0.038	0.057	-0.157	-0.037
	(0.042)	(0.048)	(0.056)	(0.161)	(0.115)
italy_dummy	0.110	-0.750	-1.079*	1.115***	0.050
	(0.329)	(0.457)	(0.654)	(0.335)	(0.511)
re_dummy	-0.112	1.600***	-1.082***	-0.115	-2.331***
	(0.317)	(0.418)	(0.383)	(0.360)	(0.776)
CONSTANT	-0.856	-2.170	-0.500	-0.452	-0.685
	(1.053)	(1.447)	(2.281)	(1.240)	(1.940)
Peusdo R^2	0.034	0.129	0.056	0.056	0.156

4.5   Conclusion

This study synthesizes a unique transaction database of 476 NPL deals during the period 2012 to 2018. Decomposition of this data enables deeper understanding about the secondary market for loan sales under distress, which so far lacks transparency and publicly available information on a broad basis. Following the financial crises of the past decade, financial institutions in the European bank-based system are still in the restructuring process of bad assets and effectively hold large portfolios of NPL on their balance sheets. Our analysis has regulatory implication, as the ECB currently ascribes the NPL-issue high priority, assisting with a variety of guidance measures. In particular since 2014, the core advice is active portfolio reduction, that requires banks to sell their oftentimes real estate-based NPL holdings to loan investors, thus resulting in a strengthening of the secondary loan sale market.

The descriptive analysis reveals that the sell-side of the secondary market is relatively granular, while we face narrow buy-side structures. While smaller single-name transactions or portfolio baskets start with smaller GBVs of €5m, the largest transactions amount up to €26bn face value. These large block transactions oftentimes account for NPL disposal into bad-banks or similar government endowed entities. Based on GBV, two thirds of the collateral (66.1%) are real estate loans. The other third accounts for consumer loans (5.7%), corporate loans (4.0%), and mixed loan pools (24.2%), which represent a mixture of the other three loan types in an unknown proportion. For this reason, we estimate the actual real estate proportion to be higher. Real estate and mixed loan pools together pinpoint the dominant role of real estate collateral in the European distressed loan sale market. Thus, the price setting for NPL portfolios is largely driven by tangible assets whose cash flow depends on rental income and property sales proceeds.

Recent empirical evidence raises doubts about the ability of financial market participants to generate information efficient valuations for real estate capital market instruments. We contribute to this stream of literature with the empirical examination of value implications for a subset of 317 NPL divestiture announcements at 58 listed banks during 2012 to 2018. Our results provide robust evidence in favor of a significant positive stock market reaction at vendor banks following NPL sales, which are driven by a size effect and real estate collateral in these transactions. This finding underpins earlier (more anecdotal and non-international) results by Geiger et al. (2007) on a much broader basis and indicates that capital markets perceive the realized sales prizes to be attractive for vendors. While failing banks generally report significant proportions of NPL prior to failure or distress (Berger and DeYoung, 1997; Jin et al., 2011), the sale of non-performing assets may be interpreted as a signaling about the vendor's willingness to ensure smooth functioning after negative shocks (Granja et al., 2017). In addition, this signaling provides security holders with positive information about the banks' willingness and ability to comply with increased regulatory pressure.

In regards to a potential divergence among different types of underlying collateral, we analyze each collateral class separately, detecting an excess return driven by real estate loans. We interpret this finding as evidence that capital markets evaluate the sales of real estate NPL portfolios as comparatively more attractive, compared to other kinds of NPL portfolios, such as unsecured corporate debt. We attribute this observation to the net effect of distinct real estate attributes. Its tangibility gives both vendor and the acquirer the opportunity to estimate its intrinsic value and facilitates the evaluation compared to the appraisal of corporate or unsecured consumer debt. But real estate also demands a very distinct skillset to adequately manage important features of real estate collateral in interdisciplinary teams of practitioners, representing high opportunity costs of capital for the vendor. With the sale of NPL portfolios, these very demanding management tasks are transferred out of the vendor banks and generate new capacities for highly specialized human resources.

Last, applying cross-sectional regression analyses, we find that bank-specific characteristics such as the vendor's bad loan to total loan ratio are consistent drivers of abnormal returns, providing evidence in favor of a size effect concerning relative asset scaling. This finding undermines recent research in the banking literature, suggesting that banks are generally incentivized to sell loans to meet their (short-term) liquidity needs under the Basel III regime, either by raising capital or reducing the amount of risk-weighted assets (Boudriga et al., 2009; Irani and Meisenzahl, 2017). As a consequence, bank capitalization is altered in favor of the capital adequacy ratio, making bank's balance sheets more appealing to the security holder (Kwan and Eisenbeis, 1997). Along this line of reasoning, the alteration is most accentuated if vendors decide to liquidate relevant portions of problematic assets. Finally, performing logistic regressions, we are also able to detect that real estate NPLs to a large extent are acquired by opportunity funds, and tend to be avoided by consortia of multiple buyers and undisclosed investors, potentially reflecting reduced opportunity costs of capital. We attribute this finding to the specific knowledge and human resources needed by investors to cope with real estate as an asset class.

Chapter 5

Concluding Remarks

This chapter provides a summary of the thesis' main findings, integrates these in the broader picture of financial market research, and delivers a final conclusion.

© Der/die Autor(en) 2021
B. C. Müller, *Three Essays on Empirical Asset Pricing in International Equity Markets*, Gabler Theses,
https://doi.org/10.1007/978-3-658-35479-4_5

Despite being of fundamental economic and scientific importance, international financial markets have remained considerably underresearched until today. This thesis presents three essays on empirical asset pricing in international equity markets. In the first essay, the role of firm-specific characteristics is analyzed for the momentum effect to exist. The second essay investigates the validity, persistence, and robustness of the newly discovered capital share growth factor across international markets as proposed by Lettau et al. (2019) for the U.S. market. Lastly, the third and final essay studies stock market reactions of vendor banks to distressed loan sale announcements. The three dissertation studies are briefly summarized as follows.

The first essay, exemplified within Chapter 2, focuses on the momentum effect which is a prominent and well-established return anomaly describing the tendency of recent past winner stocks to outperform recent past loser stocks over three to twelve months holding periods (Jegadeesh and Titman, 1993). The presented study provides a comprehensive and thorough analysis on whether this effect is more pronounced among firms that exhibit specific characteristics, as for instance younger and smaller firms. The empirical analysis relies upon 35 equity markets across the globe between January 1989 and June 2019 as well as upon 18 firm-specific characteristics. Applying rolling regressions, the set of chosen firm characteristics is used to predict momentum at the firm level. The analysis reveals that predicted momentum profits are highly significant in explaining and enhancing actually observed momentum returns. Global differences in both, ordinary and characteristics-enhanced momentum returns are found to most likely originate from cultural attributes as for instance individualism or power distance. These results make rational explanations of momentum less likely but rather provide empirical support for overreaction-based behavioral theories.

The second essay, presented within Chapter 3, analyzes whether growth in the capital share of aggregate income can explain international equity portfolio returns as proposed by Lettau et al. (2019) for the U.S. market. Given that multiple recent academic studies have emphasized data mining concerns in the field of empirical asset pricing (Cochrane, 2011; Harvey et al., 2016; Harvey, 2017), broad replications and out-of-sample tests for newly reported asset pricing factors are of specific importance. The second dissertation study therefore implements an analysis of 45 equity markets between January 1989 and December 2017 to analyze the validity, persistence, and robustness of the capital share growth factor. Following the two-step regression approach by Lettau et al. (2019), the empirical evidence presented in the study corroborates the importance of capital share growth as a local risk factor across international markets. However, the findings simultaneously imply that there exists severe geographic heterogeneity in the explanatory power of this factor. Pooled estimates show that capital share growth is particularly significant for Emerging Markets, while being less relevant for G7 + Australia (excl. U.S.). Also, and unlike the results reported by Lettau et al. (2019) for the U.S. market, information contained in the KS factor of international markets does not subsume information contained in alternative factor models, but partly adds additional explanatory content to these model specifications. Cross-country differences are found to originate from differences in private wealth inequality as well as differences in public wealth and public reserves. Overall, the study illustrates the importance of this newly discovered asset pricing factor and disperses potential data mining concerns.

The third essay, presented within Chapter 4, studies how stock markets react upon distressed loan sale announcements. To do so, the study is the first to synthesize a large transaction database which compiles 476 NPL deals of European vendor banks during the period 2012 to 2018. This data set is used to provide novel insights into the NPL market which so far lacks transparency and publicly available information. Applying event study methodology, the empirical evidence demonstrates that distressed loan sale announcements cause significant positive stock market reactions of vendor banks involved within these transactions. Information related to NPL sale announcements is priced within the [-5; +5] event window, implying that there exists only a small time horizon for investors to gain abnormal returns. Cross-sectional regression analysis further reveals that abnormal returns are driven by a size effect and real estate collateral. Lastly, applying logistic regression analysis, the study demonstrates that real estate collateralized NPLs are most often acquired by opportunistic funds, while they are avoided by consortia of multiple buyers and undisclosed investors. Overall, the study concludes that reported findings are caused by the specific characteristics of real estate as an asset class and the knowledge and human resources needed by investors to cope with it.

The three essays presented within this dissertation as well as their summarized main findings are integrated into the broader picture of financial market research as follows.

First, this dissertation contributes to the ongoing market efficiency debate by demonstrating that existing return anomalies are at least partially persistent, predictable, and most likely driven by behavioral biases. The findings reported in the first essay provide empirical support for the behavioral finance approach by Shiller (2003) and stand in contrast to the efficient market hypothesis by Fama (1970). Conversely, however, the third dissertation study shows that despite the existence of behavioral-driven return anomalies, financial market participants are still capable to accurately process highly complex information in a comparatively fast, however not immediate, manner. Apparently, this inference corroborates the rationality of financial market participants and in doing so the theory by Fama (1970). Taken together, results derived from the first and third dissertaion studies imply that both, rationality and irrationality is found to be prevalent within international equity markets.

Second, the thesis shows that despite the presence of severe data mining concerns in financial market research, newly discovered asset pricing factors offer the possibility to enhance and deepen our understanding of what drives security prices. Simultaneously, this implies that financial market research is still distant from understanding which factors truly matter in explaining expected asset returns. Broad replications and out-of-sample tests are necessary and can best be achieved upon the basis of international equity markets. This approach simultaneously augments the existing knowledge of what segments and integrates financial markets and offers the possibility to improve regulatory frameworks and market conditions, to identify cross-country differences in investor behavior, and to exploit and improve investment strategies.

Overall, it can be concluded that standard financial market theory based upon the rationality of agents is still pervasive. This thesis, however, finds that international equity markets are at least to some extent inefficient. Existing inefficiencies, in turn, seem to be driven by behavioral biases. Ultimately, the market (in-)efficiency debate as well as the search for factors explaining asset prices in a complete and robust manner goes on.

Chapter 6

Bibliography

Abowd, J. M. (1989). The Effect Of Wage Bargains On The Stock Market Value Of The Firm. *American Economic Review*, 79(4):774–800.

Adelino, M., Schoar, A., and Severino, F. (2016). Loan Originations and Defaults in the Mortgage Crisis: The Role of the Middle Class. *The Review of Financial Studies*, 29(7):1635–1670.

Albuquerue, R. and Wang, N. (2008). Agency Conflicts, Investment, and Asset Pricing. *The Journal of Finance*, 63(1):1–40.

Alvaredo, F., Chancel, L., Piketty, T., Saez, E., and Zucman, G., editors (2018). *World Inequality Report 2018*. Belknap Press.

Amihud, Y. (2002). Illiquidity and Stock Returns: Cross-Section and Time-Series Effects. *Journal of Financial Markets*, 5:31–56.

Arena, M., H. K. S. and Yan, X. (2008). Price Momentum and Idiosyncratic Volatility. *Financial Review*, 43:159–190.

Asness, C. S. (1997). The Interaction of Value and Momentum Strategies. *Financial Analysts Journal*, 53:29–36.

Asness, C. S., Moskowitz, T. J., and Pedersen, L. H. (2013). Value and Momentum Everywhere. *The Journal of Finance*, 68:929–985.

© Der/die Autor(en) 2021
B. C. Müller, *Three Essays on Empirical Asset Pricing in International Equity Markets*, Gabler Theses,
https://doi.org/10.1007/978-3-658-35479-4

Avramov, D., Cheng, S., and Hameed, A. (2016). Time-Varying Liquidity and Momentum Profits. *Journal of Financial and Quantitative Analysis*, 51(6):1897–1923.

Avramov, D. and Chordia, T. (2006). Asset Pricing Models and Financial Market Anomalies. *The Review of Financial Studies*, 19(3):1001–1040.

Avramov, D., Chordia, T., Jostova, G., and Philipov, A. (2007). Momentum and Credit Rating. *The Journal of Finance*, 62:2503–2520.

Baker, M. and Wurgler, J. (2007). Investor Sentiment in the Stock Market. *Journal of Economic Perspectives*, 21:129–151.

Ball, R. and Brown, P. (1968). An Empirical Evaluation of Accounting Income Numbers. *Journal of Accounting Research*, 6(2):159–178.

Bandarchuk, P. and Hilscher, J. (2013). Sources of Momentum Profits: Evidence on the Irrelevance of Characteristics. *Review of Finance*, 17:809–845.

Banerjee, S., Kaniel, R., and Kremer, I. (2009). Price Drifts as an Outcome of Differences in Higher-Order Beliefs. *The Review of Financial Studies*, 22:3707–3734.

Barberis, N., Shleifer, A., and Vishny, R. (1998). A Model of Investor Sentiment. *Journal of Financial Economics*, 49:307–343.

Barker, C. A. (1956). Effective Stock Splits. *Harvard Business Review*, 34(1):101–106.

Barniv, R., Hope, O. K., Myring, M., and Thomas, W. B. (2010). International Evidence on Analyst Stock Recommendations, Valuations, and Returns. *Contemporary Accounting Research*, 27(4):1131–1167.

Barroso, P. and Santa-Clara, P. (2015). Momentum Has Its Moments. *Journal of Financial Economics*, 116:111–120.

Basak, S. and Cuoco, D. (1998). An Equilibrium Model with Restricted Stock Market Participation. *The Review of Financial Studies*, 11(2):309–341.

Beck, R., Jakubik, P., and Piloiu, A. (2015). Key Determinants of Non-Performing Loans: New Evidence from a Global Sample. *Open Economies Review*, 26(3):525–550.

Bekaert, G. and Harvey, C. R. (2002). Research in Emerging Markets Finance: Looking to the Future. *Emerging Markets Review*, 3:429 448.

Bekaert, G. and Harvey, C. R. (2017). Emerging Equity Markets in a Globalizing World. *Unpublished Working Paper*.

Bekaert, G., Harvey, C. R., Lundblad, C. T., and Siegel, S. (2011). What Segments Equity Markets? *The Review of Financial Studies*, 24(12):3841 3890.

Berger, A. N. and DeYoung, R. (1997). Problem Loans and Cost Efficiency in Commercial Banks. *Journal of Banking & Finance*, 21(6):849 870.

Berk, J. B., Green, R. C., and Naik, V. (1999). Optimal Investment, Growth Options, and Security Returns. *The Journal of Finance*, 54:1553 1607.

Beugelsdijk, S. and Frijns, B. (2010). A Cultural Explanation of the Foreign Bias in International Asset Allocation. *Journal of Banking and Finance*, 34(9):2121 2131.

Bhojraj, S. and Swaminathan, B. (2006). Macromomentum: Returns Predictability in International Equity Indices. *The Journal of Business*, 79:429 451.

Binder, J. (1998). The Event Study Methodology Since 1969. *Review of Quantitative Finance and Accounting*, 11(2):111 137.

Boehmer, E., Musumeci, J., and Poulsen, A. B. (1991). Event-Study Methodology Under Conditions of Event-Induced Variance. *Journal of Financial Economics*, 30(2):253 272.

Boudriga, A., Boulila, N., and Jellouli, S. (2009). Banking Supervision and Nonperforming Loans: A Cross-Country Analysis. *Journal of Financial Economic Policy*, 1(4):286 318.

Brennan, M. J. and Xia, Y. (2001). Assessing Asset Pricing Anomalies. *The Review of Financial Studies*, 14(4):905 942.

Breuer, W. and Nadler, C. (2012). Real Estate and Real Estate Finance as a Research Field - An International Overview. *Zeitschrift für Betriebswirtschaft*, 82(S1):5 52.

Bris, A., Goetzmann, W. N., and Zhu, N. (2007). Efficiency and the Bear: Short Sales and Markets around the World. *The Journal of Finance*, 62(3):1029 1079.

Brooks, R. and Del Negro, M. (2005). Country versus Region Effects in International Stock Returns. *The Journal of Portfolio Management*, 31(4):67–72.

Brown, D. T., James, C. M., and Mooradian, R. M. (1994). Asset Sales by Financially Distressed Firms. *Journal of Corporate Finance*, 1(2):233–257.

Brown, S. J. and Warner, J. B. (1980). Measuring Security Price Performance. *Journal of Financial Economics*, 8(3):205–258.

Burq, F. and Chancel, L. (2020). Inequality Transparency Index. *World Inequality Lab Technical Note. Retrieved from https://wid.world/.*

Campbell, J. Y., Hilscher, J., and Szilagyi, J. (2008). In Search of Distress Risk. *The Journal of Finance*, 63(6):2899–2939.

Carhart, M. M. (1997). On Persistence in Mutual Fund Performance. *The Journal of Finance*, 52(1):57–82.

Carrieri, F., Chaieb, I., and Errunza, V. (2013). Do Implicit Barriers Matter for Globalization? *The Review of Financial Studies*, 26(7):1694–1739.

Chan, K., Covrig, V., and Ng, L. (2005). What Determines the Domestic Bias and Foreign Bias? Evidence from Mutual Fund Equity Allocations Worldwide. *The Journal of Finance*, 60(3):1495–1534.

Chan, L. K., Jegadeesh, N., and Lakonishok, J. (1996). Momentum Strategies. *The Journal of Finance*, 51:1681–1713.

Chen, H. J., Kacperczyk, M., and Ortiz-Molina, H. (2011). Labor Unions, Operating Flexibility, and the Cost of Equity. *Journal of Financial and Quantitative Analysis*, 46(1):25–58.

Chordia, T. and Shivakumar, L. (2002). Momentum, Business Cycle, and Time-varying Expected Returns. *The Journal of Finance*, LVII(985-1019).

Chui, A. C., Titman, S., and Wei, K. J. (2010). Individualism and Momentum Around the World. *The Journal of Finance*, 65(1):361–392.

Cici, G., Corgel, J., and Gibson, S. (2011). Can Fund Managers Select Outperforming REITs? Examining Fund Holdings and Trades. *Real Estate Economics*, 39(3):455–486.

Clubb, C. and Stouraitis, A. (2002). The Significance of Sell-Off Profitability in Explaining the Market Reaction to Divestiture Announcements. *Journal of Banking & Finance*, 26(4):671–688.

Cochrane, J. (2009). *Asset Pricing: Revised Edition*. Princeton University Press.

Cochrane, J. H. (2011). Presidential Address: Discount Rates. *The Journal of Finance*, 66(4):1047–1108.

Comment, R. and Jarrell, G. A. (1995). Corporate Focus and Stock Returns. *Journal of Financial Economics*, 37(1):67–87.

Conrad, J. and Kaul, G. (1998). An Anatomy of Trading Strategies. *The Review of Financial Studies*, 11:489–519.

Cooper, M. J., Gulen, H., and Schill, M. J. (2008). Asset Growth and the Cross-Section of Stock Returns. *The Journal of Finance*, 63:1609–1651.

Corrado, C. J. (2011). Event Studies: A Methodology Review. *Accounting and Finance*, 51(1):207–234.

Corrado, C. J. and Zivney, T. L. (1992). The Specification and Power of the Sign Test in Event Study Hypothesis Tests Using Daily Stock Returns. *Journal of Financial and Quantitative Analysis*, 27(3):465–478.

Da, Z., Gurun, U. G., and Warachka, M. (2014). Frog in the Pan: Continuous Information and Momentum. *The Review of Financial Studies*, 27:2171–2218.

Dahiya, S., Puri, M., and Saunders, A. (2003). Bank Borrowers and Loan Sales: New Evidence on the Uniqueness of Bank Loans. *Journal of Business*, 76(4):563–582.

Daniel, K., Hirshleifer, D., and Subrahmanyam, A. (1998). Investor Psychology and Security Market Under- and Overreactions. *The Journal of Finance*, 53:1839–1885.

Daniel, K., Hirshleifer, D., and Sun, L. (2020). Short- and Long-Horizon Behavioral Factors. *The Review of Financial Studies*, 33(4):1673–1736.

Daniel, K. and Moskowitz, T. J. (2016). Momentum Crashes. *Journal of Financial Economics*, 122:221–247.

Danthine, J. and Donaldson, J. B. (2002). Labour Relations and Asset Returns. *The Review of Economic Studies*, 69(1):41–64.

De Long, J. B., Shleifer, A., Summers, L. H., and Waldmann, R. J. (1990). Noise Trader Risk in Financial Markets. *The Journal of Political Economy*, 98:703–738.

Dechow, P. M., Sloan, R. G., and Soliman, M. T. (2004). Implied Equity Duration: A New Measure of Equity Risk. *Review of Accounting Studies*, 9:197–228.

Demirgüç-Kunt, A. and Levine, R., editors (2004). *Financial Structure and Economic Growth: A Cross-Country Comparison of Banks, Markets, and Development.* MIT press.

Dick, M. (2010). *Der Verkauf von Non Performing Loans: eine Analyse von NPL-Transaktionen aus Bankensicht.* Springer-Verlag.

Dimitrios, A., Helen, L., and Mike, T. . (2016). Determinants of Non-Performing Loans: Evidence from Euro-Area Countries. *Finance Research Letters*, 18:116–119.

Docherty, P. and Hurst, G. (2018). Investor Myopia and the Momentum Premium Across International Equity Markets. *Journal of Financial and Quantitative Analysis*, 53(6):2465–2490.

Dolley, J. C. (1933). Characteristics and Procedure of Common-Stock Split-Ups. *Harvard Business Review*, 11(3):316–326.

Dominguez, K. M., Hashimoto, Y., and Ito, T. (2012). International Reserves and the Global Financial Crisis. *Journal of International Economics*, 88(2):388–406.

ECB (2017). Guidance to Banks on Non-Performing Loans. *Retrieved from https://www.bankingsupervision.europa.eu.*

ECB (2018a). Introductory Statement to the Press Conference on the ECB Annual Report on Supervisory Activities 2016 (with Q&A) [Press Release]. *Retrieved from https://www.bankingsupervision.europa.eu.*

ECB (2018b). Second Ordinary Hearing in 2018 at the European Parliament's Economic and Monetary Affairs Committee [Press Release]. *Retrieved from https://www.bankingsupervision.europa.eu.*

ECOFIN (2018). Banking Union: Council Endorses Package of Measures to Reduce Risk [Press Release]. *Retrieved from https://www.consilium.europa.eu.*

Faa, L. C. (2019). The Effects of Non-Performing Loans Disposals on Banks' Stock Prices: Evidence from Italy. *POLITESI Digital Archive of PhD and Post Graduate Theses.*

Fama, E. F. (1970). Efficient Capital Markets: A Review of Theory and Empirical Work. *The Journal of Finance,* 25:383–417.

Fama, E. F. (2014). Two Pillars of Asset Pricing. *American Economic Review,* 104(6):1467–1485.

Fama, E. F., Fisher, L., Jensen, M. C., and Roll, R. (1969). The Adjustment of Stock Prices to New Information. *International Economic Review,* 10(1):1–21.

Fama, E. F. and French, K. R. (1993). Common Risk-Factors in the Returns on Stocks and Bonds. *Journal of Financial Economics,* 33(1):3–56.

Fama, E. F. and French, K. R. (1996). Multifactor Explanations of Asset Pricing Anomalies. *The Journal of Finance,* 51(1):55–84.

Fama, E. F. and French, K. R. (2012). Size, Value, and Momentum in International Stock Returns. *Journal of Financial Economics,* 105(3):457–472.

Fama, E. F. and French, K. R. (2015). A Five-Factor Asset Pricing Model. *Journal of Financial Economics,* 116(1):1–22.

Fama, E. F. and French, K. R. (2017). International Tests of a Five-Factor Asset Pricing Model. *Journal of Financial Economics,* 123(3):441–463.

Fama, E. F. and MacBeth, J. D. (1973). Risk, Return, and Equilibrium: Empirical Tests. *The Journal of Political Economy*, 81:607–636.

Favilukis, J. (2013). Inequality, Stock Market Participation, and the Equity Premium. *Journal of Financial Economics*, 107(3):740–759.

Feenstra, R. C., Inklaar, R., and Timmer, M. (2015). The Next Generation of the Penn World Table. *American Economic Review*, 105(10):3150–3182.

Fell, J., Grodzicki, M., Krušec, D., Martin, R., and O'Brien, E. (2017). Overcoming Non-Performing Loan Market Failures with Transaction Platforms. *ECB Financial Stability Review November 2017*.

Ferris, S. P., Jayaraman, N., and Sabherwal, S. (2013). CEO Overconfidence and International Merger and Acquisition Activity. *Journal of Financial and Quantitative Analysis*, 48(1):137–164.

Gallo, J. G., Lockwood, L. J., and Rutherford, R. C. (2000). Asset Allocation and the Performance of Real Estate Mutual Funds. *Real Estate Economics*, 28(1):165–184.

Gande, A. and Saunders, A. (2012). Are Banks Still Special When There Is a Secondary Market for Loans? *The Journal of Finance*, 67(5):1649–1684.

Geiger, F., Rottke, N. B., and Schiereck, D. (2007). Marktreaktionen auf Portfolioverkäufe-Transaktionen Not leidender Immobiliendarlehen in Deutschland. *Zeitschrift für immobilienwirtschaftliche Forschung und Praxis*, H(3):15–16.

Gentgen, J. (2007). *Strategien deutscher Banken: Der Umgang mit immobiliengesicherten Problemkrediten (Vol. 3)*. Springer-Verlag.

George, T. J. and Hwang, C.-Y. (2004). The 52-Week High and Momentum Investing. *The Journal of Finance*, 59:2145–2176.

Ghosh, A. (2015). Banking-Industry Specific and Regional Economic Determinants of Non-Performing Loans: Evidence from US States. *Journal of Financial Stability*, 20:93–104.

Giannetti, M. and Koskinen, Y. (2010). Investor Protection, Equity Returns, and Financial Globalization. *Journal of Financial and Quantitative Analysis*, 45(1):135–168.

Gomez, M. (2017). Asset Prices and Wealth Inequality. *Unpublished Working Paper*.

Granja, J., Matvos, G., and Seru, A. (2017). Selling Failed Banks. *The Journal of Finance*, 72(4):1723–1784.

Green, J., Hand, J. R. M., and Zhang, X. F. (2017). The Characteristics that Provide Independent Information about Average U.S. Monthly Stock Returns. *The Review of Financial Studies*, 2017:4389–4436.

Greenwald, D. L., Lettau, M., and Ludvigson, S. C. (2014). Origins of Stock Market Fluctuations. *National Bureau of Economic Research Working Paper No. 19818*.

Griffin, J. M. (2002). Are the Fama and French Factors Global or Country Specific? *The Review of Financial Studies*, 15(3):783–803.

Griffin, J. M., Hirschey, N. H., and Kelly, P. J. (2011). How Important Is the Financial Media in Global Markets? *The Review of Financial Studies*, 24(12):3941–3992.

Griffin, J. M., Ji, X., and Martin, J. S. (2003). Momentum Investing and Business Cycle Risk: Evidence from Pole to Pole. *The Journal of Finance*, 58:2515–2547.

Grinblatt, M. and Han, B. (2005). Prospect Theory, Mental Accounting, and Momentum. *Journal of Financial Economics*, 78:311–339.

Grinblatt, M. and Keloharju, M. (2001). How Distance, Language, and Culture Influence Stockholdings and Trades. *The Journal of Finance*, 56(3):1053–1073.

Guo, H. (2004). Limited Stock Market Participation and AssetPrices in a Dynamic Economy. *Journal of Financial and Quantitative Analysis*, 39(3):495–516.

Guvenen, F. (2009). A Parsimonious Macroeconomic Model for Asset Pricing. *Econometrica*, 77(6):1711–1750.

Hail, L. and Leuz, C. (2006). International Differences in the Cost of Equity Capital: Do Legal Institutions and Securities Regulation Matter? *Journal of Accounting Research*, 44(3):485–531.

Harvey, C. R. (2017). Presidential Address: The Scientific Outlook in Financial Economics. *The Journal of Finance*, 72(4):1399–1440.

Harvey, C. R., Liu, Y., and Zhu, H. (2016). ... and the Cross-Section of Expected Returns. *The Review of Financial Studies*, 29(1):5–68.

Hau, H. (2011). Global versus Local Asset Pricing: A New Test of Market Integration. *The Review of Financial Studies*, 24(12):3891–3940.

Heaton, J. and Lucas, D. (2000). Portfolio Choice and Asset Prices: The Importance of Entrepreneurial Risk. *The Journal of Finance*, 55(3):1163–1198.

Hillert, A., Jacobs, H., and Müller, S. (2014). Media Makes Momentum. *The Review of Financial Studies*, 27:3467–3501.

Hirsch, B. T. (1991). Union Coverage and Profitability Among U.S. Firms. *The Review of Economics and Statistics*, 73(1):69–77.

Hoberg, G. and Phillips, G. M. (2018). Text-Based Industry Momentum. *Journal of Financial and Quantitative Analysis*, 53(6):2355–2388.

Hofstede, G. (2001). *Culture's Consequences: Comparing Values, Behaviors, Institutions, and Organizations Across Nations*. Sage Publication, Beverly Hills, CA.

Hofstede, G. (2011). Dimensionalizing Cultures: The Hofstede Model in Context. *Online Readings in Psychology and Culture, Unit 2*.

Hofstede, G., Hofstede, G. J., and Minkov, M. (2010). *Cultures and Organizations: Software of the Mind*. New York: McGraw-Hill, 3rd edition.

Hollstein, F. (2020). Local, Regional, or Global Asset Pricing? *Journal of Financial and Quantitative Analysis, forthcoming*.

Hong, H., Lim, T., and Stein, J. C. (2000). Bad News Travels Slowly: Size, Analyst Coverage, and the Profitability of Momentum Strategies. *The Journal of Finance*, 55:265–295.

Hong, H. and Stein, J. C. (1999). A Unified Theory of Underreaction, Momentum Trading, and Overreaction in Asset Markets. *The Journal of Finance*, 54:2143–2184.

Hou, K., Chen, X., and Zhang, L. (2020a). Replicating Anomalies. *The Review of Financial Studies*, 33(5):2019–2133.

Hou, K., Karolyi, G. A., and Kho, B.-C. (2011). What Factors Drive Global Stock Returns? *The Review of Financial Studies*, 24(8):2527–2574.

Hou, K., Mo, H., Xue, C., and Zhang, L. (2020b). An Augmented q-factor Model with Expected Growth. *Review of Finance*.

Hou, K., Peng, L., and Xiong, W. (2006). R^2 and Price Inefficiency. *Unpublished Working Paper*.

Hou, K., Xue, C., and Zhang, L. (2015). Digesting Anomalies: An Investment Approach. *The Review of Financial Studies*, 28(3):650–705.

Huang, W. H., Schwienbacher, A., and Zhao, S. (2012). When Bank Loans Are Bad News: Evidence from Market Reactions to Loan Announcements Under the Risk of Expropriation. *Journal of International Financial Markets Institutions & Money*, 22(2):233–252.

Irani, R. M. and Meisenzahl, R. R. (2017). Loan Sales and Bank Liquidity Management: Evidence from a U.S. Credit Register. *The Review of Financial Studies*, 30(10):3455–3501.

Jacobs, H. and Müller, S. (2018). ... And Nothing Else Matters? On the Dimensionality and Predictability of International Stock Returns. *Unpublished Working Paper*.

Jacobs, H. and Müller, S. (2020). Anomalies Across the Globe: Once Public, No Longer Existent? *Journal of Financial Economics*, 135(1):213–230.

Jacobs, H., Regele, T., and Weber, M. (2016). Expected Skewness and Momentum. *Unpublished Working Paper*.

James, C. (1987). Some Evidence on the Uniqueness of Bank Loans. *Journal of Financial Economics*, 19(2):217–235.

Jegadeesh, N. and Titman, S. (1993). Returns to Buying Winners and Selling Losers: Implications for Stock Market Efficiency. *The Journal of Finance*, 48:65–91.

Jegadeesh, N. and Titman, S. (2001). Profitability of Momentum Strategies: An Evaluation of Alternative Explanations. *The Journal of Finance*, 56:699–720.

Jiang, G., Lee, C. M., and Zhang, Y. (2005). Information Uncertainty and Expected Returns. *Review of Accounting Studies*, 10(2-3):185–221.

Jin, J. Y., Kanagaretnam, K., and Lobo, G. J. (2011). Ability of Accounting and Audit Quality Variables to Predict Bank Failure During the Financial Crisis. *Journal of Banking & Finance*, 35(11):2811–2819.

John, K. and Ofek, E. (1995). Asset Sales and Increase in Focus. *Journal of Financial Economics*, 37(1):105–126.

Johnson, T. C. (2002). Rational Momentum Effects. *The Journal of Finance*, 57:585–608.

Julliard, C. (2007). Labor Income Risk and Asset Returns. *Unpublished Working Paper*.

Karolyi, A. G. (2016). Home Bias, an Academic Puzzle. *Review of Finance*, 20(6):2049–2078.

Karolyi, G. A. and Wu, Y. (2014). Size, Value, and Momentum in International Stock Returns: A New Partial-Segmentation Approach. *Unpublished Working Paper*.

Keeton, W. R. and Morris, C. S. (1987). Why Do Banks' Loan Losses Differ? *Economic Review*, 72(5):3–21.

Keynes, J. M. (1936). *The General Theory of Employment, Interest and Money*. Macmillan, London, UK.

Klein, M. (2013). Non-Performing Loans in CESEE : Determinants and Impact on Macroeconomic Performance. *IMF Working Paper No. 13/72*.

Kothari, S. P. and Warner, J. B. (2007). *Handbook of Empirical Corporate Finance*. Elsevier.

Krause, T., Sondershaus, T., and Tonzer, L. (2017). Complexity and Bank Risk During the Financial Crisis. *Economics Letters*, 150:118–121.

Kurtzman, J., Yago, G., and Phumiwasana, T. (2004). The Global Costs of Opacity. *MIT Sloan Management Review*, 46(1):38–45.

Kwan, S. and Eisenbeis, R. A. (1997). Bank Risk, Capitalization, and Operating Efficiency. *Journal of Financial Services Research*, 12(2-3):117–131.

La Porta, R., Lopez-de-Silanes, F., Shleifer, A., and Vishny, R. W. (1997). Legal Determinants of External Finance. *The Journal of Finance*, 52(3):1131–1150.

Lasfer, M. A., Sudarsanam, P. S., and Taffler, R. J. (1996). Financial Distress, Asset Sales, and Lender Monitoring. *Financial Management*, 25(3):57–66.

Laudenbach, C., Malmendier, U., and Niessen-Ruenzi, A. (2020). The Long-Lasting Effects of Living under Communism on Attitudes towards Financial Markets. *NBER Working Paper*.

Lee, C. M. and Swaminathan, B. (2000). Price Momentum and Trading Volume. *The Journal of Finance*, 55:2017–2069.

Lettau, M., Ludvigson, S. C., and Ma, S. (2019). Capital Share Risk in U.S. Asset Pricing. *The Journal of Finance*, 74(4):1753–1792.

Leuz, C., Nanda, D., and Wysocki, P. D. (2003). Earnings Management and Investor Protection: An International Comparison. *Journal of Financial Economics*, 69(3):505–527.

Lewellen, J. (2002). Momentum and Autocorrelation in Stock Returns. *The Review of Financial Studies*, 15:533–564.

Lewellen, J. (2015). The Cross Section of Expected Stock Returns. *Critical Finance Review*, 4:1–44.

Lewellen, J., Nagel, S., and Shanken, J. (2010). A Skeptical Appraisal of Asset Pricing Tests. *Journal of Financial Economics*, 96:175–194.

Lewis, K. K. (2011). Global Asset Pricing. *Annual Review of Financial Economics*, 3:435–466.

Li, J. (2018). Explaining Momentum and Value Simultaneously. *Management Science*, 64(9):4239–4260.

Lintner, J. (1965). Valuation of Risk Assets and the Selection of Risky Investments in Stock Portfolios and Capital Budgets. *The Review of Economics and Statistics*, 47(1):13–37.

Lintner, J. (1969). The Valuation of Risk Assets and the Selection of Risky Investments in Stock Portfolios and Capital Budgets: A Reply. *The Review of Economics and Statistics*, 51(2):222–224.

Louzis, D. P., Vouldis, A. T., and Metaxas, V. L. (2012). Macroeconomic and Bank-Specific Determinants of Non-Performing Loans in Greece: A Comparative Study of Mortgage, Business and Consumer Loan Portfolios. *Journal of Banking & Finance*, 36(4):1012–1027.

Lustig, H. and Van Nieuwerburgh, S. (2008). The Returns on Human Capital: Good News on Wall Street Is Bad News on Main Street. *The Review of Financial Studies*, 21(5):2097–2137.

MacKinlay, A. C. (1997). Event Studies in Economics and Finance. *Journal of Economic Literature*, 35(1):13–39.

Maio, P. and Philip, D. (2018). Economic Activity and Momentum Profits: Further Evidence. *Journal of Banking and Finance*, 88:466–482.

Makarov, I. and Rytchkov, O. (2012). Forecasting the Forecasts of Others: Implications for Asset Mispricing. *Journal of Economic Theory*, 147:941–966.

Malloy, C. J., Moskowitz, T. J., and Vissing-Jørgensen, A. (2009). Long-Run Stockholder Consumption Risk and Asset Returns. *The Journal of Finance*, 64(6):2427–2479.

Mankiw, N. G. and Zeldes, S. P. (1991). The Consumption of Stockholders and Nonstockholders. *The Journal of Financial Economics*, 29(1):97–112.

Maskara, P. K. and Mullineaux, D. J. (2011). Information Asymmetry and Self-Selection Bias in Bank Loan Announcement Studies. *Journal of Financial Economics*, 101(3):684–694.

McLean, R. D. and Pontif, J. (2016). Does Academic Research Destroy Stock Return Predictability? *The Journal of Finance*, 71(1):5–32.

Menkhoff, L., Sarno, L., Schmeling, M., and Schrimpf, A. (2012). Currency Momentum Strategies. *Journal of Financial Economics*, 106:660–684.

Min, B. K. and Kim, T. S. (2016). Momentum and Downside Risk. *Journal of Banking and Finance*, 72:104–118.

Mori, M. and Ziobrowski, A. J. (2011). Performance of Pairs Trading Strategy in the U.S. REIT Market. *Real Estate Economics*, 39(3):409–428.

Moskowitz, T. J. and Grinblatt, M. (1999). Do Industries Explain Momentum? *The Journal of Finance*, 54:1249–1290.

Myers, J. H. and Bakay, A. J. (1948). Influence of Stock Split-Ups on Market Price. *Harvard Business Review*, 26(2):251–255.

Pennacchi, G. G. (1988). Loan Sales and the Cost of Bank Capital. *The Journal of Finance*, 43(2):375–396.

Petzev, I., Schrimpf, A., and Wagner, A. F. (2016). Has the Pricing of Stocks Become More Global? *BIS Working Papers*.

Portes, R. and Rey, H. (2005). The Determinants of Cross-Border Equity Flows. *Journal of International Economics*, 65(2):269–296.

Rapach, D. E., Strauss, J. K., and Zhou, G. (2013). International Stock Return Predictability: What Is the Role of the United States? *The Journal of Finance*, 68(4):1633–1662.

Rizova, S. (2010). Predictable Trade Flows and Returns of Trade-Linked Countries. *Annual Meeting of the American Finance Association*.

Rottke, N. and Gentgen, J. (2008). Workout Management of Non-Performing Loans. *Journal of Property Investment & Finance*, 26(1):59–79.

Rouwenhorst, K. G. (1998). International Momentum Strategies. *The Journal of Finance*, 53:267–284.

Sagi, J. S. and Seasholes, M. S. (2007). Firm-Specific Attributes and the Cross-Section of Momentum. *Journal of Financial Economics*, 84:389–434.

Salas, V. and Saurina, J. (2002). Credit Risk in Two Institutional Regimes: Spanish Commercial and Savings Banks. *Journal of Financial Services Research*, 22(3):203–224.

Schneider, F., Buehn, A., and Montenegro, C. E. (2010). New Estimates for the Shadow Economies all over the World. *International Economic Journal*, 24(4):443–461.

Sharpe, W. F. (1964). Capital Asset Prices: A Theory of Market Equilibrium Under Conditions of Risk. *The Journal of Finance*, 19(3):425–442.

Shiller, R. J. (2003). From Efficient Markets Theory to Behavioral Finance. *Journal of Economic Perspectives*, 17(1):83–104.

Shilling, J. and Wurtzebach, C. (2012). Is Value-Added and Opportunistic Real Estate Investing Beneficial? If So, Why? *Journal of Real Estate Research*, 34(4):429–461.

Shleifer, A. and Vishny, R. W. (1997). The Limits of Arbitrage. *The Journal of Finance*, 52:35–55.

Stambaugh, R. F. and Yuan, Y. (2017). Mispricing Factors. *The Review of Financial Studies*, 30(4):1270–1315.

Thaler, R. (2005). *Preface in: Advances in Behavioral Finance, Volume II.* Princeton University Press.

The Nobel Foundation (2021). All Prizes in Economic Sciences. *Retrieved from https://www.nobelprize.org/.*

Vayanos, D. and Woolley, P. (2013). An Institutional Theory of Momentum and Reversal. *The Review of Financial Studies*, 26:1087–1145.

Verardo, M. (2009). Heterogeneous Beliefs and Momentum Profits. *Journal of Financial and Quantitative Analysis*, 44:795–822.

Viale, A. M., Kolari, J. W., and Fraser, D. R. (2009). Common Risk Factors in Bank Stocks. *Journal of Banking & Finance*, 33(3):464–472.

Watanabe, A., Xu, Y., Yao, T., and Yu, T. (2013). The Asset Growth Effect: Insights from International Equity Markets. *Journal of Financial Economics*, 108(2):529–563.

Whalen, G. (1991). A Proportional Hazards Model of Bank Failure: An Examination of Its Usefulness as an Early Warning Tool. *Economic Review*, 27(1):21–31.

Woltering, R. O., Weis, C., Schindler, F., and Sebastian, S. (2018). Capturing the Value Premium - Global Evidence from a Fair Value-Based Investment Strategy. *Journal of Banking & Finance*, 86:53–69.

You, H. and Zhang, X. J. (2009). Financial Reporting Complexity and Investor Underreaction to 10-K Information. *Review of Accounting Studies*, 14(4):559–586.

Zhang, M. B. (2019). Labor-Technology Substitution: Implications for Asset Pricing. *The Journal of Finance*, 74(4):1793–1839.

Zhang, X. F. (2006). Information Uncertainty and Stock Returns. *The Journal of Finance*, 61:105–137.